THE GREAT DEBATE ON BANKING REFORM

THE GREAT DEBATE ON BANKING REFORM

NELSON ALDRICH AND THE ORIGINS OF THE FED

Elmus Wicker

The Ohio State University Press
Columbus

Library of Congress Cataloging-in-Publication Data

Wicker, Elmus.
The great debate on banking reform : Nelson Aldrich and the origins
of the Fed / Elmus Wicker.—1st ed.
    p. cm.
Includes bibliographical references and index.
ISBN 0–8142–1000–7 (cloth : alk. paper)—ISBN 0–8142–9078–7
(cd-rom) 1. Board of Governors of the Federal Reserve System (U.S.)—
History. 2. Monetary policy—United States—History. 3. Banking law—
United States. 4. Banks and banking—United States—History. 5.
Aldrich, Nelson W. (Nelson Wilmarth), 1841–1915. I. Title.
    HG2563.W46 2005
    332.1'1'0973—dc22
                                2005004639

Cover design by Dan O'Dair.
Type set in Adobe Garamond.
Printed by Thomson-Shore, Inc.

The paper used in this publication meets the minimum requirements
of the American National Standard for Information Sciences—
Permanence of Paper for Printed Library Materials. ANSI Z39.48–1992.

9 8 7 6 5 4 3 2 1

CONTENTS

ILLUSTRATIONS

FIGURES

TABLE

PREFACE

The story of the origins of the Fed needs revision. The canonical account identified Representative Carter Glass of Virginia as the "father" of the Federal Reserve System, who in collaboration with his legislative assistant H. Parker Willis drafted the Glass-Owen bill that eventually emerged as the Federal Reserve Act. Panic prevention was its main objective, and the real bills doctrine the guide for Fed policymakers. Each of the three propositions is deeply embedded in the literature on the origins of the Fed; each warrants reconsideration. Senator Nelson Aldrich of Rhode Island deserves equal billing with Carter Glass as a cofounder of the Fed. Panic prevention had been achieved in the Aldrich-Vreeland bill (1908). Moreover, the Federal Reserve Act was real bills neutral! Another study of the origins of the Fed should be welcome if these revisions can be supported by the available evidence. Setting the record straight needs no further justification.

The debate on banking reform can for expositional purposes be divided into three separate but slightly overlapping stages between 1894 and 1913. The first stage produced a variety of proposals for an asset-based currency, permitting participating banks to issue currency on the basis of a bank's general assets. Agreement was reached eventually in 1908 on a measure that made provision for an asset-based currency with commercial paper as the backing for use solely during emergencies. The key words are temporary and emergency. The Aldrich-Vreeland Act remained on the books until 1914, when it expired. By that time more permanent banking reform measures would presumably have been enacted. The act provided for the appointment of a National Monetary Commission for the specific purpose of studying and making concrete recommendations for permanent banking reform. No one had any definite ideas about what the commission might accomplish. Thus ended the first stage of the movement for banking reform.

The second stage opened with the New York Chamber of Commerce's proposal for a central bank in 1906 and Paul Warburg's plan for a central bank in the following year. However, no one in the first half of 1908 thought a central bank would be at the top of the banking reform agenda. Senator Nelson Aldrich had rejected the idea as premature. Asset-based currency proposals monopolized the banking reform debate, but not for much longer. By the end of the summer, as a consequence of the National Monetary Commission's visit to Europe, Aldrich became a convert to the new viewpoint. The whole complexion of the debate changed. Thereafter, a central bank was the only proposal on the table. The transition from an asset-based currency to a central bank was abrupt and dramatic. Together with a small, elite group of young Wall Street bankers, Senator Aldrich arranged a clandestine meeting at Jekyll Island, Georgia in November 1910 from which emerged an early draft of what later was labeled the Aldrich bill, which called for the creation of a U.S. style central bank even though every effort was made to avoid the label. The Aldrich bill was stillborn, having received no support in the Senate, thus ending the second stage of the movement for banking reform.

The demise of the Aldrich bill initiated the third and final stage of debate on banking reform. Leadership passed from Aldrich to Representative Carter Glass of Virginia. Glass became chairman of the House Banking and Currency Committee and with the sanction of the newly elected President Woodrow Wilson began work immediately preparing a Democrat-sponsored bill with a central bank as its chief focus.

The first two stages I have labeled the Great Debate, for it was during this period that two options were available: an asset-based currency and a central bank. And further progress toward the establishment of a central bank could not proceed until that debate had run its course. Thereafter, the debate was less interesting, for it was mainly concerned with technical details, that is, structural and organizational characteristics of a new central bank.

The Federal Reserve was not the United States's first experiment in central banking. Both the First and Second Banks of the United States preceded the Fed. But their demise left a traumatic residue that was one of the chief obstacles to the creation of a U.S. central bank. At the beginning of the Great Debate on banking reform in 1894, public opposition to a central bank was a political fact of life. The abandonment of this shibboleth was a precondition for the establishment of a central bank. Senator Aldrich and his associates deserve credit for having removed this obstacle as a deterrent to a favorable reception of the idea of a U.S. style central bank. Aldrich's victory made it possible for the debate to continue with only one issue in mind—what kind of central bank?

My interest in the Federal Reserve goes back almost forty years. While the Fed was preparing to celebrate its fiftieth anniversary, the Federal

Reserve Board was giving consideration to making their archival records available to qualified scholars. By coincidence, I just happened to have submitted a request to examine their records at about the same time. The Board approved my request, and I was the first outsider to whom the records were made available without restriction. I was able to get on with the task of writing a history of Federal Reserve monetary policy from 1917 to 1933. In the process of writing the book, I repeatedly encountered questions relating to the origins of the Fed, which I set aside for another time. The same questions reappeared while at work on my next two books, on banking panics of the Great Depression and the Gilded Age. Not wanting to postpone the task any longer, I began work on this book.

Until quite recently our chief source of information on the origins of the Fed was H. Parker Willis (1923), who as an associate of Glass was responsible for drafting a bill. For reasons that are not altogether clear, historians have shown little interest in the Fed. But that lack of interest has been dispelled by the recent studies of Livingston (1986) and McCulley (1992), whose works are distinguished by the extensive use of the papers of the leading participants in the banking reform debate, especially that part of the debate that culminated in the Aldrich-Vreeland bill and the Aldrich bill.

The weakness of both the Livingston and McCulley studies is the lack of critical judgment. The reader after working her way through a host of banking reform proposals is given no basis for appraising their economic viability. For example, one learns neither whether the Aldrich-Vreeland bill was an effective panic-preventive measure nor whether there were sound economic reasons for believing an asset-based currency issued by the banks was an effective remedy for banking panics.

Political scientists have discovered the Fed as well. Broz (1997) attributed the origins of the Fed to the desire of New York bankers to make the dollar an international currency and end our dependence on Europe to finance our export trade. Timberlake (1984), Tallman and Moen (2001), and Toma (1997) have also contributed novel explanations of the origins of the Fed. The so-called origins of the Fed problem is a research problem of some significance.

I have undertaken a long, interpretive essay with the intent of revising the conventional explanation for the origins of the Fed. A clearer idea of the origins of the Fed may contribute to understanding Federal Reserve behavior, especially in the earlier years. Whether it does or not, however, is not especially relevant. To repeat, setting the record straight is reason sufficient.

I wish to acknowledge helpful comments received on individual chapters from Anna Schwarz, Alan Meltzer, Ellis Tallman, Perry Mehring, and

CHAPTER ONE

THE GREAT DEBATE: AN OVERVIEW

The movement for banking reform in the United States after the Civil War was motivated by frequent bouts of acute monetary stringency and less frequent banking panics. The financial and economic distress accompanying the disturbances was the trigger that set off a debate on banking reform that took place in three overlapping stages between 1894 and 1913, an interval just short of twenty years. The former date coincided with the so-called Baltimore Plan presented to the American Bankers Association (ABA) and the latter with the passage of the Federal Reserve Act. Proposals for an asset-based currency issued by the participating banks dominated the first stage from 1894 to 1908 that culminated in the passage of a temporary measure known as the Aldrich-Vreeland Act. The need for and viability of a U.S.-style central bank monopolized the second and third stages and ended with the creation of the Federal Reserve System in 1913.

These periodic bouts of monetary stringency and banking panics were attributed to alleged defects in the national banking system. The stock of currency did not respond to seasonal increases in demand associated with the planting of crops in May and their harvesting in October. Increased demands for currency in the interior had to be met by drawing down banker balances in New York, usually attended by varying degrees of monetary stringency, curtailment of loans to the stock market, and spikes in interest rates. Nor did the currency stock respond to panic-induced demands for currency which provoked a suspension of cash payments.

The note issue of the national banks was described as "inelastic," a term that became embedded in the banking reform literature. The incentive to increase the supply of national bank notes depended solely on the price of eligible government bonds. Banks could issue notes up to 90 percent of the par or market value of the bonds purchased. The higher the price, the weaker the incentive to purchase. For example, a bank purchasing an eligible bond with a par value of $1,000 and selling for $1,500 could issue $900 of bank notes. As the price rose it became increasingly more expensive for the bank to issue notes. And there was no good reason for expecting bond prices to behave in such a way to ensure seasonal and panic elasticity.

The diagnosis, if correct, led to a legislative remedy in the form of an asset-based currency. National banks should be permitted to issue notes against their general assets. The bond-secured currency of the National Banking Act was asset-based, but it was restricted to a single asset. General assets included commercial paper, railroad bonds, U.S. government bonds, and bonds of state and local governments.

What, if anything, would limit the note issue on the basis of general assets? At the one extreme were the real bills advocates, who argued that the note issue would be self-liquidating and required no constraints if confined to self-liquidating commercial paper. But legislators were more pragmatic and less doctrinaire; they recommended limiting the note issue to the amount of the issuing bank's capital stock and made provision for a guaranty fund to protect the note holders of failed banks. When reasons were given for imposing constraints on the note issue, the fears of overissue usually came first. The smaller banks could not be trusted to exercise the proper caution and restraint.

The appeal of an asset-based currency resided in its simplicity. It did not require further intrusion by government into the banking industry. No major institutional changes were necessary. And it would impart the desired liquidity to meet seasonal and panic demands. However, it was a remedy for a double defect, the occurrence of banking panics and seasonal money market stringency. Multiple defects might require multiple solutions.

Although an asset-based currency was the preferred remedy proposed during the first stage of the debate on banking reform, other solutions were not ignored. Branch banking and deposit insurance were given thoughtful consideration. Less attention was paid to reserve pooling by the New York Clearing House banks. Frequently between 1894 and 1902 asset-based currency proposals were coupled with branch banking. Both the McClary (1898) and the Fowler (1902) bills contained branch banking provisions. Livingston (1986, p. 80) maintained that "branch banking became an integral part of the reform agenda once serious discussions of assets currency had begun." Combining the two would presumably concentrate reserves and tend to equalize regional interest rates. European and Canadian banking experience had demonstrated the close relationship between a highly centralized banking structure, branch banking, and banking stability. A further concentration of financial power through nationwide branch banking was, however, politically unacceptable and would remain so for another 100 years.

So much attention had been paid to making the note issue safe, scarcely any concern was shown about the safety of deposits, but that began to change after the 1907 panic. Eight states passed laws guaranteeing bank deposits. The idea was not new. An 1829 banking law required banks to contribute annually to a fund that could be used to repay the holders of notes and deposits. The Populist party revived the deposit guarantee proposals in the 1890s. The 1908 Democratic platform contained a plank establishing a deposit insurance scheme for national banks. Thereafter, the guarantee of deposits gained in popularity, but it was a rise that only strengthened the opposition of the nation's bankers.

A fourth solution to the banking panic problem was advanced by O. M. W. Sprague (1910), who argued that the New York Clearing House had the power, the tools, and the knowledge to prevent banking panics. Reserve pooling among the NYCH banks had successfully averted banking panics in 1860 and 1861, but had not successfully done so in 1873, for reasons I have explained elsewhere (Wicker, 2000). Thereafter the NYCH abandoned reserve pooling, and by 1893 it had all but been forgotten. Sprague's mentor at Harvard, Charles Dunbar (1891), kept alive the NYCH experience with reserve pooling.

The pace of the banking reform movement accelerated after the 1907 financial panic. Congress responded in 1908 with the Aldrich-Vreeland bill, a temporary stopgap measure until a permanent reform measure could be adopted. To expedite the transition, the Aldrich-Vreeland bill called for the appointment of a National Monetary Commission to study and make recommendations for comprehensive banking reform. While the commission was deliberating, the Aldrich-Vreeland bill would fill the gap. The bill provided for an emergency currency based on both a bond-secured and asset-based currency, mainly commercial paper. There was only one occasion in August 1914, the outset of World War I, when the provisions of the bill as amended were successfully invoked to forestall an incipient banking panic. Aldrich-Vreeland effectively brought an end to the first stage of the debate on banking reform.

Three events signaled the onset of the second stage: a New York Chamber of Commerce report in1906, Paul Warburg's publication of a plan for a central bank in 1907, and the appointment of the National Monetary Commission in 1908. The commission was not a blue ribbon panel of experts who would study the current banking system and make recommendations for permanent banking reform. Its eighteen members were legislators, nine of whom were from the House of Representatives and nine from the Senate, with Senator Nelson Aldrich as the chairman. He was mindful of the challenging task before him and the payoff of "enduring fame" if he were successful. His six terms in the U.S. Senate had brought him to the apex of political power. Among Republicans, he had no rival. Firmly ensconced in his leadership role, Aldrich was reluctant to share power with others. Used to getting his own way, he kept a tight rein on the agenda and proceedings of the commission. According to the commission's director of research it was a "one man show" completely dominated by Aldrich. Members of the commission played a purely ancillary role, though Aldrich was attentive to maintaining their trust and support.

One of the very best kept secrets in U.S. financial history, at least until 1930, was that the Aldrich bill was not drawn up by the Monetary Commission but by a secret cabal of New York bankers who at the invitation of Aldrich met at a Jekyll Island lodge off the coast of Georgia in November 1910 and prepared a rough draft outline of what later became the Aldrich bill for the creation of a U.S. style central bank. The participants included representatives of three of the largest Wall Street banks: Henry Davison, a Morgan partner, Frank Vanderlip a vice-president of National City Bank and a protégée of James Stillman, and Paul Warburg, partner in Kuhn, Loeb, and Co., two of whom had gone on record as advocates of a central bank. What was more irregular was the presence of A. Piatt Andrew, former assistant professor at Harvard, who had been recruited by Aldrich to serve as special assistant to the commission but who at the time of the Jekyll Island conclave was assistant secretary of the treasury. His participation was not known to his boss, Secretary of the Treasury Franklin MacVeagh, or to anyone else in the Taft administration. Only Senator Aldrich could have conceived such a daring and risky plan. Only Aldrich had the audacity and wit to carry it out knowing quite well what the consequences would be if found out.

What emerged at Jekyll Island was not a completed draft of a banking reform bill. It was presented to the commission without the knowledge of its origins as a suggested plan for monetary legislation. The plan was dated January 16, 1911 and revised subsequently in October. The final report of the commission was sent to the Senate in January 1912 without any action being taken. The Aldrich bill was the seed that eventually became the Federal Reserve Act, and that seed had been planted by Aldrich and his banker associates, a striking triumph of dynamic leadership and dogged persistence.

To establish a central bank in the United States at least three formidable obstacles had to be overcome, the first of which was the shibboleth against a central bank—a carryover from the antebellum dispute between Andrew

Jackson and Nicholas Biddle about the renewal of the charter of the Second Bank of the United States. No progress could be made toward the creation of a central bank until this nationwide prejudice was either removed or significantly moderated. The second obstacle was a banking reform measure that had gained wide appeal between 1894 and 1908, the so-called asset-based currency whereby individual banks would be allowed to issue paper currency using commercial paper as its principal backing. Deposits and notes would thereby be interconvertible. The third obstacle was the almost complete absence of strong congressional leadership of the banking reform movement before 1908. There was no dearth of banking reform proposals, none of which, however, could muster enough congressional support. The story of the origins of the Federal Reserve System can be told by explaining how each of these three obstacles was successfully removed.

Two lawmakers, one of whom we have already mentioned, played leading roles in the creation of a U.S. style central bank: Senator Nelson Aldrich of Rhode Island and Representative Carter Glass of Virginia. Aldrich and his associates were responsible for removing the first two obstacles. Glass and Aldrich shared the congressional leadership role, Aldrich between 1908 and 1912 and Glass thereafter.

As a joint sponsor of the Aldrich-Vreeland bill (1908) Aldrich reluctantly agreed to allow participating banks to issue emergency currency backed by commercial paper for the purpose of forestalling banking panics. As chairman of the National Monetary Commission, he rejected the Aldrich-Vreeland solution and opted for a central bank in a dramatic reversal.

Carter Glass, the so-called "father" of the Federal Reserve Act, and Parker Willis, his close associate, went out of their way to repudiate Aldrich's influence, but it is now becoming increasingly clear that Aldrich deserves equal, if not top, billing with Glass as a cofounder of the Federal Reserve System. The claim that Aldrich's contribution has been understated is based on the following considerations:

1. The Aldrich-Vreeland Act was an effective panic-preventive measure; it successfully forestalled an incipient banking panic in August 1914.
2. Aldrich was chiefly responsible for shifting the debate on banking reform from an asset-based currency to that of a central bank.
3. Aldrich alone among American politicians and statesmen had the courage, guile, and political power to disavow the deeply ingrained prejudice against a central bank.
4. The similarity in substance and wording of the Aldrich and the Glass-Owen bills was striking.

5. The nationwide educational campaign launched by Aldrich and his associates to publicize the idea of a central bank did more than perhaps anything else to increase public support for a central bank.

Although the Aldrich bill's introduction in the Senate in January 1912 proved to be stillborn, the foundations laid by Senator Aldrich accelerated progress on a new banking reform measure. The debate no longer centered on whether or not to have a central bank but on what kind of central bank. The principal task of Carter Glass was to formulate a revised banking bill which could be steered successfully through the Congress. And that was the extent of Glass's legislative achievement. Aldrich prepared the way by winning the debate on whether or not to have a central bank and removing the shibboleth against a central bank. The achievement of Glass can no longer be considered separately from that of Aldrich and his associates.

The reassessment of the role of Aldrich may require alternative interpretations of the origins of the Federal Reserve. The conventional wisdom has it that the Fed was created to prevent banking panics. Had panic prevention been the predominant motive, there would have been no need to go beyond the Aldrich-Vreeland bill. A close comparison of the Aldrich and the Glass-Owen bills reveals, contrary to the conventional wisdom, that they were both real bills neutral. There is nothing in either act to warrant a strong real bills interpretation, which is to say that looking after the quality of credit, the quantity will look after itself. A real bills interpretation has been inferred primarily from the views of Glass and Willis, but mainly Willis. At least three of the five persons who drafted the Aldrich bill rejected the real bills doctrine as fallacious. Nevertheless, despite the contrary interpretations of Glass and Willis and Aldrich and his associates, they were able to agree on the same discount provision in the two bills.

The central unifying theme of the book is a reconsideration, reappraisal, and revival of an old claim that Senator Nelson Aldrich deserves recognition as a cofounder of the Federal Reserve System. Each of the following chapters bears directly on that claim. The exception is Chapter 2, which provides the reader with an update on recent contributions to the origins of the Fed literature. Chapters 2 through 5 define what the Great Debate was about. A variety of asset-based currency proposals for banking reform between 1894 and 1906 are the subject of Chapter 3. A separate chapter, Chapter 4, is devoted to the Aldrich-Vreeland bill (1908), which served two purposes: it settled the debate about a preferred asset-based currency plan, and it created a National Monetary Commission to consider a permanent solution to the problem of banking reform. Chapter 5 introduces the other side of the debate between advocates of an asset-based currency and a central bank. A plan for a U.S. style central bank emerged from a clandestine meeting convened by Senator Aldrich and including a cabal of Wall Street bankers in the form of an early outline of what became known as the Aldrich bill. When introduced in Congress, the Aldrich bill went nowhere, and leadership passed to Representative Carter Glass, who almost immediately began work on a substitute bill. The Glass bill is the subject of Chapter 6. A comparison of the two bills is set out in Chapter 7. The comparison is continued in Chapter 8 with the examination of the theoretical underpinnings of the two bills in the form of the real bills doctrine. The concluding chapter, Chapter 9, sums everything up.

CHAPTER TWO

RECENT LITERATURE REVISITED

The revival of interest in the origins of the Federal Reserve System has been an exciting scholarly development. With the exception of West's (1977) study, the topic had lain dormant since the 1920s. Part of the revival has been purely accidental; it coincided with the works of two historians, James Livingston (1986) and Richard McCulley (1992), and a political scientist Lawrence Broz (1997). Previously, neither historians nor political scientists had paid any attention to the origins of the Fed question. Economists' interest was also reawakened; they were attracted to explanations of the origins of the Fed with the underpinnings in the private clearinghouse association within a self-regulating framework. The initial sparks have ignited a whole new research agenda.

The U.S. problem had been to get bankers to take action, especially during banking panics, that would benefit all as members of a group but might not be thought to be consistent with their individual self-interest. A solution to the collective action problem seemed to reside in the clearinghouse, a voluntary association of banks originally created to expedite the clearing and collection of checks, but which subsequently provided the only opportunity for organized cooperation among the participating banks. Collective action by the New York Clearing House was responsible for forestalling banking panics in 1860 and 1861 (and less successfully in 1873) by agreeing to the equalization or pooling of reserves among the NYCH banks. Thereafter, reserve pooling in a crisis was abandoned for lack of support and was never revived. Banks with surplus funds were reluctant to aid banks with a deficit of funds. Self-interest crowded out collective action.

In the absence of effective collective action, solutions were sought to the inelastic currency and banking panic problems that focused on the individual bank motivated solely by self-interest. This class of banking reform proposals was asset-based. Currency issued by individual banks chartered by the comptroller of the currency (national banks) had been bond-secured; that is, a national bank could issue paper currency upon the purchase of eligible government securities. Advocates of banking reform from 1894 to 1908 were dissatisfied with a bond-secured currency for reasons that will become clearer later and substituted an asset-based currency on commercial paper. The amount of currency each participating bank could issue was constrained to a proportion of its capital stock. Moreover, a guaranty fund protected noteholders of failed banks. The safeguards against overissue did not satisfy everyone. There remained the threat that small local banks would overissue and thus generate inflation. Asset-based currency proposals were the immediate forerunners of a U.S. style central bank. Any inquiry into the origins of the Fed necessarily entails a detailed account of the various proposals and their legislative success or failure.

We begin by summarizing the work of the two historians: James Livingston (1986) and Richard McCulley (1992), and then we take up the contribution of J. Lawrence Broz (1997), a political scientist. We then turn to the contributions of the economists: Mark Toma (1997), Gary Gorton and Donald Mullineaux (1987), Richard Timberlake (1984), and Ellis Tallman and Jon Moen (2001). We begin with a short summary of their contributions and then turn to a more extended discussion.

Our knowledge of the movement for banking reform has been considerably enhanced during the past fifteen years by the three major studies of Livingston (1986), McCulley (1992), and Broz (1997). Both Livingston and Broz have advanced original interpretations of the Fed's origins. Livingston, a neoprogressive (Marxist), attributed the Fed's origins to the concentration of ownership and control of the modern corporation which, he thought, required a centralization of financial responsibility in the guise of a central bank. Broz also called attention to the structural changes taking place in the American economy after 1870. The growth of the U.S. share of world trade required the "internationalization of the dollar." Before 1913 the dollar was not an international currency, and the financing of exports and imports was in the hands of foreign bankers. To gain an increased share of world trade, New York bankers needed to spearhead a movement for banking reform which necessitated also a reform of the payments mechanism.

Although less original than Livingston or Broz, McCulley (1992) set his historical narrative in a broader political context, illustrating how sectional and economic interests together with political and partisan clashes shaped the course of banking reform. He did not think the origins of the

Fed were to be found in purely economic considerations; that is, in structural weaknesses of the national banking system. Banking reform may have originated in frequent banking panics and seasonal money market stringency, but something more was required if banking reform was to succeed.

Namely, bankers and businessmen had to be aroused, to be followed later by a well-mobilized public opinion to ensure a favorable legislative response by the politicians. The task was formidable and required patience, self-discipline, and, more importantly, experienced leadership. McCulley's study is the best organized of the three. Although there are no original hypotheses or startling revisions of interpretation, his scholarship is sound and his judgment mature, which gives the narrative a tone of authority missing in Broz and Livingston.

What distinguished each of the three from earlier treatments of the origins of the Fed is the extensive use of manuscript collections including those of Glass, Willis, Aldrich, Warburg, Vanderlip, and Laughlin, as well as others. McCulley and Livingston are the first historians, to my knowledge, to have attempted a serious and extended treatment of the origins of the Fed. Neither economists nor economic historians of money and banking had taken the pains to explore the archival sources. West (1977) was the exception; he acknowledged the use of the papers of Willis, Strong, and Laughlin, but no others.

McCulley and Livingston fill an important gap in the literature on the origins of the Fed by describing the progress of banking reform from the mid-1880s until the passage of the Federal Reserve Act in 1913. For example, we have full descriptions of what happened at the Indianapolis Monetary Convention in 1896, the proposals presented to the American Bankers Association at various intervals, the evolution of the Aldrich-Vreeland Act (1908), and the Aldrich bill (1912). Proposals for banking reform such as branch banking, deposit insurance, asset-based currency, and a central bank are described fully. By the time of the appointment of the National Monetary Commission in 1908 various banking reform proposals with the exception of a central bank had been thoroughly canvassed, at least between bankers and business leaders. What was absent was any progress toward reconciling the various remedies. A catalyst was missing. And no group was able to exert strong leadership to eliminate these differences.

Various remedies for the elimination of banking panics were on the table: branch banking, deposit insurance, and the like, but they were regarded as politically infeasible. An asset-based currency issued by the national banks had been rejected by the New York bankers. The reserve pooling remedy of the NYCH had been forgotten.

JAMES LIVINGSTON

Livingston's interpretation of the origins of the Fed is Marxist inasmuch as the prime mover was a so-called business elite, a ruling class who were committed to remaking capitalism in the United States. The concepts of class and class-consciousness explain the emergence of a ruling class. Although the phrasing is recognizably Marxian, the language turns out to be extraneous to the events being described. It is the facts being described rather than the interpretation imparted to them that lend merit to Livingston's study.

He is the first historian to have systematically utilized the papers of the leading participants in the post-1870 movement for banking reform. Moreover, he has provided a detailed description of the main issues and events associated with the banking reform movement from 1870 to 1913. His account of the movement for banking reform in the United States begins well before the Aldrich-Vreeland Act and the creation of the National Monetary Commission in 1908. By that date considerable progress had been made in identifying the alleged weaknesses of the national banking system, in suggesting remedies, and in educating the general public about the necessity for banking reform. But there was still a long way to go. No consensus had been reached about what ought to be done. Both the corporate and banking sectors exercised initiative in mobilizing opinion within each sector and provoking discussion about the various remedies. In these endeavors the American Bankers' Association (ABA) and the New York Chamber of Commerce, as well as the Indianapolis Monetary Convention, deserve special recognition.

Among the issues drawing the most attention were an asset-based currency, branch banking, deposit insurance, and a central bank. The ABA had recommended the Baltimore Plan in 1894 for the issue of currency on the basis of general assets of the banks. The report of the Indianapolis Monetary Commission in 1896 also recommended an asset currency coupled with a proposal for branch banking. Livingston maintained that until 1902 the movement for banking reform centered on the recommendations of the Indianapolis Monetary Commission. The Fowler bill of the same year added a branch banking provision.

The Livingston narrative established how far the debate had progressed by 1907 on the necessity of an asset-based currency, the establishment of some form of central bank, and the mobilization of corporate and business opinion on the merits of banking reform. He identified the leaders who were in the forefront of pre-1907 banking reform, Frank Vanderlip, A. Hepburn, J. Laughlin, J. Forgan, Lyman Gage, and many others, and evaluated their contributions.

Livingston attempted to show how a corporate business elite organized the movement for banking reform and constituted its social basis. This sentence could stand equally well if the word "elite" were removed; he documented how business leaders mobilized public opinion and orchestrated the movement for banking reform. The novelty of Livingston's interpretation does not reside in its Marxian underpinnings but in two controversial hypotheses he advanced to explain the movement for banking reform and the creation of a central bank: (1) the controlling assumption of the reform agenda after 1893 was that the banking sector had countercyclical responsibilities; and (2) concentration and control of the new corporate business sector required a corresponding centralization of responsibility in a central bank. He proposed the first hypothesis to explain the movement for banking reform which began in the early 1890s. It coincided with a serious economic depression and shaped the outlook of businessmen and bankers who were seeking remedies for the economic malaise. Currency reform, he thought, was a countercyclical solution. Without a central bank, the banking sector had the responsibility for maintaining effective demand; specifically, he meant the expansion of bank lending. The recognition of these responsibilities would be enhanced if legislation were enacted removing the tax on the issue of state bank notes, legalizing clearinghouse certificates, and allowing banks to issue an asset-based currency.

The Livingston hypothesis placed banking reform in the broader context of the business cycle, in sharp contrast to a narrower framework of seasonal movement of interest rates and banking panics. The implicit assumption never stated was that currency reform would provide a device for moderating cyclical changes in economic activity, and that was the motivating objective of the reformers. The weak link in the chain, however, is the relationship between smoothing interest rates, eliminating banking panics, and moderating economic contraction. Livingston attempted to demonstrate that the movement for banking reform must be viewed in the broader setting of general economic activity, and the bankers were supposed to recognize their countercyclical responsibilities.

Livingston's second hypothesis can be put in its strongest form, as follows: the existence of a growing corporate business sector implies the existence of a central bank. But he failed to provide any evidence to support that proposition. Was the existing institutional framework effective in providing for the financial requirements of an expanding corporate sector? Were the capital and money markets up to the task? The answer to the first question is far broader than the creation of a central bank. The key issue is the efficiency with which saving was channeled into investment—the intermediation process. Banks obviously play an important role in this process, but it is not at all clear why a central bank is a necessary condition for the efficiency of the intermediation process or the efficient functioning of the capital market. Livingston has not identified specific defects in the capital markets that required the intervention of a central bank.

Contrary to Livingston's assertion, heads of corporate business and bankers did not labor long and hard for a central bank, but as we shall show, for *a particular form* of central bank that was banker controlled. When President Woodrow Wilson rejected their plea for banker control, their enthusiasm turned to anger and frustration. They opposed the passage of the Glass-Owen bill. The so-called business elite and ruling class received a rude awakening. All, however, was not lost. Glass-Owen allowed New York banks to engage in the financing of the export trade. The opposition of the New York banks was noted by Willis (1923, pp. 306–7):

> 'The New York group or element in the National Citizens League which had been previously hostile to anything except the Aldrich bill, from the very beginning practically declared open war; its members employing all of the usual legislative stratagems and methods for the purpose of defeating the Federal Reserve Act in the Senate, or at all events amending it back into conformity with the terms of the Aldrich measure.'

Livingston's exposition of the views of the leading participants in the Great Debate on banking reform is frequently marred by his literal transcription of an archaic and obsolete economic language usage in which their views were embedded. Consequently, often the reader is not able to make heads or tails of the validity of the issue being contested. And Livingston refrains from either translating the language into current jargon or attempting to evaluate the validity of the archaic argument.

J. LAWRENCE BROZ

Broz, who is a political scientist, has succeeded in producing an original interpretation of the origins of the Fed—no mean feat considering that the Federal Reserve Act is over eighty-five years old. He assigned a key role to international considerations, downplaying the conventional view that domestic factors were paramount, most notably the prevention of banking panics. Without a new international goal, he maintained, there was no plausible explanation of how the barriers to collective action were surmounted. It was the rapid advance of the American economy after 1870 that generated the requisite incentive to undertake a drastic reform of the banking system.

The dollar had no international stature, and American exporters and importers had to rely on foreign banks to finance external trade. With the rise of America's global position, these arrangements became increasingly irksome and created a demand for institutional change. The opportunity cost of the existing financial machinery in the form of lost potential revenue to American banks increased. The handful of New York banks that could take advantage of an internationalized dollar had a strong financial incentive to initiate a plan for banking reform that would enable the dollar to acquire the status of an international currency. But that entailed the overhaul of the payments machinery as well. The one could not be accomplished without the other.

To explain how the appropriate incentive structure to innovate was generated, Broz (1997, p. xi) resorted to Mancur Olson's joint products model, which he thought was the key to understanding the voluntary collective action behind the Federal Reserve Act; Broz maintained that "a public good produced jointly with a private good can yield collective action in a large group setting, because the addition of the private good creates the necessary convergence between the individual and the social costs of collective action." To put it another way: if an agent wants to produce a private good whose production is contingent on the production of the public good, it will act as the incentive to produce both goods. Internationally the dollar was the private good desired by a small group of large New York banks, and the redesign of the payments mechanism was the public good.

It was not the benefits of the elimination of banking panics that provided the motivation, but the potential gains to a few banks of revamped international monetary arrangements. That explains the key entrepreneurial role played by a small coterie of influential New York bankers selected by Aldrich that constituted the vanguard of the banking reform movement. The Federal Reserve Act was a response to the new role of the United States in the world economy, not as previously thought the answer to the domestic financial instability produced by banking panics. International considerations were the catalyst for banking reform.

Improving the role of the U.S. dollar in world trade was a well-recognized goal of both the Aldrich and the Glass-Owen bills. Broz simply elevated its priority as a motivation for creating the Federal Reserve System. But he underestimated what other powerful incentives might have motivated the New York bankers besides anticipated gains of internationalizing the dollar. Foremost among these other incentives was the desire to shape whatever changes were to be made so as to conform to the preferences of the New York banks, namely a new banking structure that would minimize outside governmental interference and prevent the creation of an asset-based currency. The New York bankers had a relatively low opinion of the knowledge available in the rest of the country on matters pertaining to banking reform; they would be loathe to surrender the initiative to the midwestern bankers or to politicians in Washington.

Why, we may ask, if international considerations were paramount, did the New York banks so strenuously oppose the Glass-Owen bill? The framework for internationalizing the dollar was not a matter of dispute. If they had achieved their primary objective, why wrangle over the control issue? After all, according to Broz, it was the benefits from dollarization that explains the incentive for change. Broz states that their public opposition to the bill was contradicted by their privately held views; that is, they thought that they could live with the bill though it left much to be desired. Nevertheless, they were prepared to sabotage the Glass-Owen bill even if they had gained their international objective. That hardly makes sense.

RICHARD McCULLEY

The third study on the origins of the Fed to be considered was also the work of a historian. He tells the story of the banking reform movement from the time of the Indianapolis Monetary Convention in 1897 to the creation of the Federal Reserve System in 1913. Unlike Livingston and Broz, there are no grand new interpretations or surprising hypotheses to reveal. The distinctiveness of his contribution resides solely in his imaginative organization of the narrative. He constructed a three-part scheme purely for narrative purposes as a device for classifying the various proposals for banking reform: Wall Street, LaSalle Street, and Main Street. Proposals emanating from New York were labeled Wall Street; those originating from the ABA, largely dominated by Chicago bankers, LaSalle Street; and from the many small town banks and local businesses, Main Street. There is much to be said for McCulley's schema, which tended to remove political and partisan differences from the spotlight and shifted the focus to regional and sectional differences instead.

In the approximately two decades before the Federal Reserve Act was passed, the weaknesses of the national banking system were fully aired and specific remedies proposed. No agreement, however, could be reached about what the preferred remedy should be. The debate had focused on the merits of a bond-secured and asset-based currency. Should all greenbacks be retired? LaSalle Street favored the retirement of U.S. notes and their replacement by an asset-based currency. The ABA authorized a currency report in 1906 which called for minimum government interference in banking and an asset-based currency. Wall Street, on the other hand, was unalterably opposed to giving individual banks the power to expand the note issue. Main Street preferred provision for the issue of emergency currency without any drastic changes in the note issue function.

McCulley identified the leading issue following the 1907 panic as the role government would play in a reformed banking system. LaSalle Street preferred self-regulation and a minimum of government control. Both LaSalle Street and Wall Street agreed that the government's role should be small, the smaller the better. But when the initiative for initiating legislation shifted to Aldrich, he assembled a group of like-minded young New York bankers to meet at Jekyll Island to draft a banking bill. McCulley's portraits of the participants revealed a group of self-confident, intelligent, and well-informed New York bankers who never doubted their credentials for the task before them. Central to the Jekyll Island concept of a central bank was autonomous banker control, that is, independent of government: "the essence of the Jekyll Island Plan was a centralized banking system that was independent of government, beyond political reach and that was banker administered in the interests of the financial community as a whole" (1992, p. 233). To McCulley this was the crucial issue. Apparently no consideration was given to a government controlled structure, although minority representation by government was debated. The priorities of the Jekyll Island group matched those of LaSalle Street and Main Street. Self-regulation was not only favored by the bankers; it was highly regarded by Carter Glass, the author of the Glass bill. It was based, however, on his commitment to the real bills doctrine. There was no need for outside regulation; credit would expand and contract with the needs of business. Glass thought that at least there should be some banker representation on the Federal Reserve Board but abandoned his position out of deference to the wishes of President Wilson, to whom banker control was anathema.

Neither Livingston nor McCulley regarded the progress of banking reform legislation through the various committees of the House and the Senate to be deserving of careful and detailed consideration. Livingston thought that it added nothing to his account of the origins of the Fed. McCulley skipped over it quickly, even though he regarded banker control the key issue; but it was the subject of extensive discussion during the debates in Congress.

McCulley's distinctive contribution resides in his description and analysis of the politics of banking reform, that is, the process of consensus formation by which a specific banking reform goal is achieved. This task is quite different from assessing the economic viability of various banking reform proposals. What was economically viable was not necessarily politically feasible. The main participants in the Great Debate included bankers, businessmen, economists, and legislators, as well as the president. A successful policy outcome turned on either reconciling or muting diverse and conflicting interests. There were marked differences between bankers and legislators. McCulley's telling metaphors—Wall Street, LaSalle Street, and Main Street—were meant to capture some of those conflicting interests. Banker opinion dominated the first stage of the debate, which was controlled by LaSalle Street and the proposal for an asset-based currency. At the beginning of the second stage Wall Street bankers seized the initiative when they recommended a central bank.

Once reform measures reached the legislative stage, purely partisan political considerations surfaced. Legislation originating with bankers and business trade associations while the debate process was in gestation was presumably nonpartisan, but legislation required a congressional sponsor, and the debate thereafter assumed a partisan tone. The partisan character of the debate became sharper when the president saw fit to exercise leadership. In 1912 the Democratic platform contained a plank expressing opposition to the Aldrich bill and a central bank. The emergence of a party agenda for banking reform came rather late in the debate. It was preceded by attempts to reach consensus among the interested parties, mainly bankers and businessmen. Congress was not reluctant to initiate legislation, but in the absence of strong support from bankers and businessmen, it could go nowhere.

ORIGINS OF THE FED: ECONOMISTS' CONTRIBUTIONS

Reawakened interest in the origins of the Fed was reflected not only in the Livingston, McCulley, and Broz studies, but also by a series of papers by Gorton (1985), Gorton and Mullineaux (1987) and Timberlake (1984), as well as a monograph by Toma (1997). Toma (1997) and Gorton (1985) advanced a novel hypothesis: that the founders of the Fed intended to create a national clearinghouse rather than a modern central bank. The national clearinghouse was supposed to compete with the private clearinghouse system. In Toma's model, public finance considerations, namely government revenue requirements, were important in predicting fundamental changes in monetary institutions. Seigniorage requirements presumably dictated the kind of banking reform. If the seigniorage requirements were large, a central bank would be preferred to the national clearinghouse arrangement, but seigniorage requirements were not significant. Toma and Gorton concluded the founders of the Fed created a competitive reserve banking system of limited national scope that was supposed to be self-regulating in accordance with the real bills doctrine. Toma acknowledged (1997, p. 30) that public finance considerations "played a relatively minor role in this political and economic debate leading up to the founding of the Fed." They were absent. It is indeed anomalous to attribute a critical role to public finance considerations even when the founders were ignorant of their own motivation! The significance of real bills influence will be addressed in a later chapter.

Timberlake (1984) believed that the creation of the Fed was partly a reaction to the discretionary policies of the secretary of the treasury, who had assumed some responsibility during banking panics by injecting government funds, especially in select New York banks. His actions had been condemned by bankers in the interior as arbitrary, having the undesired effect of holding down interest rates. Proposals had been made to turn the U.S. Treasury into a central bank, but the debate focused on other remedies, notably an asset-based currency.

Ellis Tallman and Jon R. Moen (2001) find the origins of the Federal Reserve System in the panic of 1907. Not only did the panic accelerate the banking reform movement, but it was the distinctive characteristic of that panic that converted the New York bankers to the idea of a central bank. In a series of papers (1990; 2001, p. 148) the authors have focused on the trust companies in New York as the source of the 1907 crisis. Deposits of New York City trust companies fell nearly 37 percent compared with a decline of more than 11 percent for state banks in the city, whereas the deposits of New York City national banks actually increased by over 8 percent. The banking panic in the city was a trust company panic, where the suspensions were the highest. Since the trust companies were not members of the NYCH, they were refused financial support. But there was more to it than nonmembership in the NYCH. Jealousy and rivalry among the commercial banks and the trust companies was also a factor. Although aid came eventually from a consortium of banks initiated by J. P. Morgan, the runs on the trust companies continued. Nevertheless, some of the younger generation of New York bankers—Strong, Vanderlip, and Davidson—became convinced of the necessity for a central bank. But we may very well ask why Tallman and Moen did not conclude that allowing trust company membership in the NYCH was the solution. Since the trust companies were allegedly the source of the 1907 panic, making provision for their support during banking disturbances through the clearinghouse should have solved the problem. Why the necessity for a central bank?

Earlier attempts to find a solution to the banking panic problem through the NYCH were overlooked by Gorton (1985) and Toma (1997). Although Timberlake (1984) was aware of these efforts, he objected to the equalization of reserves (reserve pooling) for two reasons: (1) due to moral hazard, the individual bank would feel no constraint in making demands on the pool; and (2) pooling was unnecessary, for banks with surplus reserves would lend to banks with deficit reserves, thereby redistributing the pool of reserves. Surplus banks, however, were not disposed to decrease their stock of legal tender to deficit banks so that they could continue to pay out currency to interior banks. Timberlake (1984) asked: "Why did we establish a central bank under government auspices when the clearinghouse system, with some modification, could have refined and continued as an effective lender of last resort?" The modification he had in mind, however, was not reserve pooling. Rather, the clearinghouse should be permitted to issue currency with a security collateral requirement. Unlike clearinghouse loan certificates, these notes would be paid out and thereby enter the general circulation. The loan certificate was a device that allowed the clearinghouse in effect to discount paper of the participating banks, the proceeds of which could be used to discharge clearinghouse indebtedness, thereby serving in a limited sense a central bank function. The issue of loan certificates did not, however, prevent interior banks from reducing their banker balances and demanding legal tender currency. These demands when unmet could lead to the suspension of cash payment by the clearinghouse banks. The clearinghouse could not issue currency, although on occasion certificates of small denomination did circulate. Suspension of cash payment was not a matter of insufficient reserves. The problem lay in the unequal distribution of these reserves among the twelve or fifteen largest New York City banks holding the majority of bankers' balances. Some of these banks had a surplus of reserves, some had a deficit. In 1860 the NYCH called for a pooling of reserves whereby specie belonging to the associated banks would be treated as a common fund for mutual aid and protection. This pooling arrangement was used successfully in 1860 and 1861 and less so in 1873.

The reserve pooling arrangement as a viable remedy for banking panics was retrieved recently by Wicker (1996) to illustrate how far the New York Clearing House and its leaders had gone in recognizing its responsibility for banking stability and creating the instrument for its implementation. Walter Bagehot was doing the same for the Bank of England at precisely the same time! The London *Economist* (Dec. 8, 1860, pp. 5–6) called the reserve pooling device "as remarkable as any which the remarkable annals of commercial panics can show, and one which removed the difficulty in a 'strange way.'" A month later (Jan. 26, 1860) it stated that reserve pooling was "an expedient view, we believe, in banking and showing their bankers great confidence in each other, the result has been entirely satisfactory." *The New York Times* (Nov. 22, 1960, p. 8) reported that the NYCH had voted to meet the crisis "primarily and boldly by unlimited expansion" by making "common their whole stock of specie now about 20 million." Currency could be paid out as long as it lasts, and if not adequate "they will go down together . . ." The *Times* acknowledged that the strategy was new, but it was the "approved and successful policy under such circumstances, of the national banks of England and France." The NYCH had recognized as early as 1858 that the associated banks in New York City were the holders of the ultimate banking reserve.

In a report (NYCH, No. 5, 1858, p. 50) prepared by George S. Coe, president of the American Exchange Bank in 1858, it was clearly acknowledged that the New York City banks were the ultimate holders of the specie reserve and "bear the same relation to this country as the Bank of England does in the United Kingdom." Moreover:

> It must always be remembered that the absence of any important central institution, such as exists in other commercial nations, the associated banks (NYCH) are the last resort in this country, in times of financial extremity, and upon their stability and sound conduct the national prosperity greatly depends.

No statement of the responsibilities of the NYCH was ever stated more clearly. Reserve pooling and the loan certificate were the instruments forged specifically for panic prevention.

After the 1873 panic no more is heard about reserve pooling. Opposition had arisen because some banks attempted, a few successfully, to evade the pooling arrangements by treating newly received greenbacks as "special deposits" which were excluded from the pool. The greenbacks were then replaced with national bank notes and paid over the counter. A policy of collective action was suppressed by the stronger rent-seeking motivation of some of the NYCH banks.

Charles F. Dunbar (1907, p. 146) and Oliver Sprague (1910), both professors of economics at Harvard University, did their utmost to keep the idea of reserve pooling alive, but they were unsuccessful. Sprague's study of banking panics of the National Banking Era for the National Monetary Commission set out very clearly and persuasively the reserve pooling policies of the NYCH in 1860 and 1861. However, there are no references in the congressional hearings and debates on the Glass-Owen bill to such an arrangement. It evaporated from the literature, which probably accounts for Gorton and Toma's omission of any discussion of this remedy.

RECAP

The brief survey of recent contributions to the origins of the Fed literature reveals the extent to which scholarly interest has been aroused. What is indeed surprising is that it includes the work of two historians and a political scientist, as well as economists. Economists might have been expected to maintain a lively interest, but why the recent burgeoning attention? We may conjecture that they were responding to the persistent and sometime strident criticism of central bank behavior by reopening the question: Are central banks really necessary? Was there a free market solution? That is no more than a step away from a rephrased question: What were the alternatives to the creation of a U.S. style central bank?

I have not been able to find an equally plausible explanation for the newly awakened interest of the historians and a political scientist. They have been Johnny-come-latelies to the operation of the Federal Reserve System. Undoubtedly they are better qualified than economists to unravel the process involved in mobilizing the relevant interest groups in banking and business to support a change to a central bank and the internal politics within the halls of Congress to develop a majority consensus for banking reform. They are less helpful on the purely technical questions of central banking. It could be said that they were merely responding to an acknowledged gap in our knowledge. The timing, however, still remains a mystery.

The Livingston-McCulley contributions leave some crucial questions unanswered. Why were asset-based currency proposals rejected in favor of a central bank? If internationalization of the dollar was the key objective of the New York bankers, why did they reject the Glass-Owen bill? What role, if any, did Senator Aldrich play in the establishment of the Federal Reserve System? Answers to these questions should be found in the chapters to follow.

CHAPTER THREE

THE QUEST FOR AN ASSET-BASED CURRENCY, 1894–1908

The quest for an asset-based currency rested on the premise that the note issue function resided with the commercial banks and not the government. The existing stock of paper currency was a hybrid: U.S. greenbacks issued during the Civil War, treasury notes of 1890, and bond-secured national bank notes. Advocates of an asset-based currency wished to extend the base to include the general assets of the banks, and not simply government bonds, with the circulation privilege. Several of the asset-based currency schemes also included provisions for the abolition of the bond-secured currency created by the National Banking Act and the redemption of the greenbacks and treasury notes of 1890. Midwestern and southern bankers and businessmen generally favored an asset-based currency, to which New York bankers objected. The hub of the dispute centered about the question of whom to trust. Those who favored an asset-based currency maintained that historical experience demonstrated that a government-sponsored currency tended to be overissued and inflationary. Those who opposed, namely New York bankers, argued that the multitude of small, rural banks could not be deterred from overissue. Regional and sectional differences were at the heart of the Great Debate on banking reform.

The reform of the paper currency was widely regarded as the solution to the problems of the National Banking System: seasonal money market stringency and banking panics. And the changes did not require more government regulation or the creation of a new financial institution in the guise of a central bank. An asset-based currency had been endorsed at the ABA's convention in 1894—the so-called Baltimore Plan. Almost simultaneously the secretary of the treasury and the comptroller of the currency submitted similar proposals. Secretary Carlisle's (1894) plan was debated extensively in the U.S. House of Representatives, but no legislative action was taken. Allowing national banks to issue their own notes on the bank's general assets reemerged as a recommendation of the Indianapolis Monetary Convention in 1898, of the ABA in 1906, and as a second best alternative of the New York Chamber of Commerce. This stage of the debate culminated with the passage of the Aldrich-Vreeland Act in 1908 permitting national banks to issue emergency currency, bond-secured or backed by commercial paper, until a permanent banking reform measure could be enacted. The Aldrich-Vreeland Act solved the problem of banking panics, but the confirmatory evidence was not forthcoming until the 1914 banking disturbance.

The occasion for the Great Debate on banking reform in the United States was an alleged defect in the national banking system, which was blamed for the post–Civil War sequence of banking panics and seasonal money market stringency. The main component of the paper currency was notes issued by government chartered banks backed by U.S. government bonds. These notes could only be issued when national banks had the incentive to purchase government securities with the circulation privilege. But the incentive rarely coincided with the increased demand for paper currency. These demands were both seasonal and panic-related. The failure of the national bank note issue to respond to these demands was labeled "inelasticity of the note issue."

The remedy, or one of the remedies, was to devise a note issue mechanism that would remove the inelasticity defect. One such device was the so-called asset-based currency, currency that is based on the general assets of a bank, not simply bond-secured assets. Each participating bank could issue its own notes based on its general assets, usually commercial paper. A tax on the note issue presumably would ensure speedy redemption and a guaranty fund to redeem the notes of failed banks.

The second stage of the Great Debate on banking reform overlapped the first and formally began on a national scale when the New York Chamber of Commerce in 1906 recommended the creation of a European style central bank. The banking panic of 1907 intervened and served as a catalyst that accelerated the timing of banking reform. Columbia University, acting upon the initiative of Professor E. R. A. Seligman, sponsored a series of nine lectures in 1907–8 the purpose of which was to provide a public forum to sharpen the focus of the discussion of banking reform. Three of the lecturers were strong advocates of a central bank: Frank Vanderlip, A. Barton Hepburn, and Paul Warburg. Warburg was the least compromising of the three. Unlike Vanderlip, he did not think an asset-based currency was a second best alternative; furthermore, he did not regard an inelastic currency as the chief defect of the national banking system. But the stage was set for serious consideration of a central bank by a provision of the Aldrich-Vreeland bill that called for the appointment of a National Monetary Commission chaired by Senator Nelson Aldrich of Rhode Island. The debate was effectively put on hold between the appointment of the commission and its final report in 1910. Thereafter, attention centered on a U.S. style central bank, and proposals for an asset-based currency were finally abandoned. Let us now turn to a full description of the various asset-based currency proposals.

THE BALTIMORE PLAN

The Baltimore Plan was a highly visible benchmark in the initial stage of the movement for banking reform. For the first time the approval of a powerful and influential interest group, the ABA, was solicited in an attempt to obtain currency reform legislation. Prior to 1894 many individual voices had been raised, but collective action by a large national constituency had been absent. Bankers of the Baltimore Clearing House presented a proposal for currency reform to the annual convention of the ABA chaired by Charles C. Homer, president of the Second National Bank of Baltimore, who submitted it for revision to A. Barton Hepburn, president of the First National Bank of New York, and Horace White, editor of the *New York Evening Post*. The Baltimore Plan thrust currency reform into the public arena, where it remained for the next twelve years. Moreover, the main provisions of the plan were repeated in all subsequent asset-based currency proposals: an asset-based currency, a bank capital constraint on the note issue, a tax on the currency issue to ensure rapid note redemption, safety and guaranty of the note issue, and a distinction between normal and emergency currency issue. Although the 1893 banking panic drew no response from Congress, some members of the banking fraternity were less willing to remain silent.

The Baltimore Plan boldly called for the elimination of a bond-secured currency provided for in the National Banking Act. In its place national banks would be allowed to issue bank notes on the basis of their general assets up to 50 percent of paid-in capital. The plan also authorized the issue of an additional emergency currency equal to 25 percent of paid-in capital. Including both the normal and the emergency note issue, each national bank could issue notes equal to a total of 75 percent of its paid-in capital. To ensure the early redemption of the normal note issue, a tax of one percent was levied on the outstanding circulation; the emergency issue would be subject to an increased rate of one and one-half percent. A guaranty fund was created to redeem the notes of failed banks. The new bank notes were not legal tender and could not be counted as part of the reserve.

The idea for the Baltimore Plan was borrowed from Canadian banking practice. It was tacitly assumed that the note issue function resided with the banks and not the government. Canada's highly concentrated banking system was composed of thirty-eight banks that issued bank notes based on the general assets of the banks. The notes were jointly guaranteed by all the participating banks and represented a first lien on all the bank's assets. The Canadian government bore no responsibility for redeeming the notes of failed banks. Although the note issue function attracted the attention of the sponsors of the Baltimore Plan, they did not overlook the branch banking aspect of the Canadian system, either.

Framers of the Baltimore Plan appear to have been preoccupied with the joint problems of safety of the note issue and fear of inflation. Answers were sought to two questions: Were note holders adequately protected against loss? And what would deter banks from overissue? They addressed the safety issue by providing for a 5 percent guaranty fund and making notes a prior lien on all the failed banks' general assets. According to Laughlin (1920, p. 28) the security of the note issue was large and unquestionable. He acknowledged that the safety of the note issue under the Baltimore Plan was superior to the existing bond-secured currency because under the plan bank notes were secured by all of the bank's assets rather than the stock of government bonds under the National Banking Act. Dangers from overissue were addressed by limiting the note issue of a single bank to a certain percentage of its paid-in capital. A capital stock constraint would presumably enable the banks to absorb the losses to note holders of the failed bank. An additional deterrent to overissue was a tax on the new currency issue at such a rate to ensure quick redemption after a crisis had passed.

Laughlin (1920, p. 26) did not think the Baltimore Plan addressed the real problem, which was not in his judgment an inelastic currency. Taking a clue from Walter Bagehot, he insisted that in time of panic what was needed was the liberal expansion of loans, and that was possible if the supply of reserves was elastic. An elastic currency, he thought, was not a remedy for an inelastic stock of reserves. And the Baltimore Plan did not address the reserve problem. He concluded that an elastic note issue was not a universal panacea for banking panics.

The Baltimore Plan was only the first in a succession of asset-based currency reform proposals whose purpose was to provide an elastic currency for purposes of panic prevention and seasonal demands. Its strength lay in the fact that banking reform could be accommodated without radical institutional change merely by substituting an asset-based currency for the bond- secured currency sanctioned by the National Banking Act. Its major weakness was an inflation fear that the note issue of individual banks—particularly small, rural banks—despite safety provision could not be adequately constrained. The Baltimore Plan failed for lack of congressional support. But it succeeded in spawning a host of similar proposals.

CARLISLE-ECKELS PROPOSALS

Two administration officials, Secretary of the Treasury John G. Carlisle (1894) and Comptroller of the Currency James H. Eckels (1894), both proposed separate versions of an asset-based currency similar to the Baltimore Plan. The Carlisle proposal, like the Baltimore Plan, called for the abolition of a bond-secured currency. National banks would be allowed to issue new bank notes on the basis of the general assets of the banks up to 75 percent of paid-in capital, the same percentage as the Baltimore Plan. No distinction, however, was made between regular and emergency issues. The distinguishing characteristic of the Carlisle proposal was the size of the guaranty fund, which amounted to 30 percent of the authorized circulation, held in the form of legal tender currency. As we shall see, its size was not related solely to safety considerations. A safety fund separate from the guaranty fund amounted to 5 percent of the outstanding circulation. If the guaranty and safety funds proved inadequate, the government could redeem the notes of failed banks out of its own funds, to be replenished from the sale of the assets of the failed banks and a tax on all national banks to rebuild the safety fund. Unlike the Baltimore Plan, the government had a positive role to play.

Comptroller of the Currency Eckels also submitted a proposal that each national bank deposit with the secretary of the treasury 50 percent of its paid-in capital stock in legal tender currency, in exchange for which the bank would receive newly issued bank notes dollar for dollar. After the deposit of the initial 50 percent, the banks with the remaining 50 percent could issue bank notes backed by the general assets of the bank and secured by a safety fund raised by a tax on the total circulation. Keeping deposits with the U.S. Treasury of 50 percent of paid-in capital would reduce by $340 million greenbacks redeemable in gold. Further redemption would be possible with surplus revenue of the Treasury. Eckels objected particularly to the government issue of bank notes on the basis that they had never been able to control the amount of the issue. Nevertheless, unlike the Baltimore Plan, the Carlisle and Eckels plans made provision for the partial retirement of greenbacks.

The three plans, Baltimore, Carlisle, and Eckels, differed in some important respects, but they were all in agreement that government should not issue currency notes and that an asset-based currency should replace the bond-secured currency of the National Banking Act. The merits of the three proposals were fully debated in over 400 pages of extensive hearings by the House Currency and Banking Committee. The Carlisle plan had been embodied in House Bill 8149. Witnesses did not confine their testimony to any of the three bills. The sponsors of the Baltimore Plan, Horace White, A. Barton Hepburn, and Charles Homer, were all called to testify, as well as the secretary of the treasury and the comptroller of the currency.

It became obvious during the hearings that the retirement of the greenbacks and treasury notes of 1890 was of equal, if not greater, importance than an asset-based note issue. All three plans regarded their retirement as crucial to currency reform but left it to the discretion of Treasury and the accident of a budgetary surplus. The two issues—an asset-based currency and the retirement of the greenbacks—could best be treated separately, though a few witnesses were adamant about giving the highest priority to greenback retirement.

The 30 percent legal tender guarantee was inserted in the Carlisle bill not so much for bank note safety considerations but to immobilize a proportion of the greenbacks and treasury notes of 1890 so that they would no longer constitute a threat to the Treasury's gold reserve. To obtain gold, the importer exchanged legal tender notes for gold at the Treasury. Instead of retiring the notes, the Treasury was required to reissue them. The Treasury held the gold reserve as a convertibility requirement for greenbacks and treasury notes of 1890. Any undue reduction in that reserve might generate expectations both here and abroad that convertibility might be suspended, a factor that contributed to the 1893 banking panic.

The stumbling blocks of the three proposals included whether or not the government should have any liability for notes of failed banks, whether state banks should be allowed to issue circulating notes, and whether bank note legislation should contain provisions for the retirement of greenbacks and treasury notes of 1890. Safety of the note issue tended to crowd out considerations of exactly how an asset-based currency would forestall banking panics; that is, was the extension of the note issue privilege to state chartered banks a precondition for panic prevention? Would national banks be reluctant to participate in the absence of compulsion? The hearings were silent about currency reform through the creation of a central bank. Currency reform was only partly a matter of the elasticity of the note issue; it was also a matter of how to maintain the convertibility of legal tender notes. The most serious objections raised in the hearings on the

Baltimore, Carlisle, and Eckels plans dealt with the note issue privilege, should it belong to government or the banks; the membership question, whether state banks should once again be allowed to issue notes; and the joint liability problem, that is, the responsibility of all participating banks to redeem the notes of failed banks.

The right-to-issue question provoked the most aggressive response. The line was sharply drawn between those who claimed the note issue privilege should be restricted solely to the banks and those who maintained that the note issue was the sole responsibility of government. The majority of the witnesses favored a bank sponsored note issue. The restoration of the note issuing privilege to state banks evoked an almost equally strong reaction. The safety and guaranty funds did not assuage the fears of those who thought the extension of the circulation privilege would tempt excessive entry of new banks.

Probably the most controversial provision of the Baltimore Plan was joint liability of participating banks in the event of the failure of a bank. They would all share in the responsibility for losses of a failed bank. Large national banks might be reluctant to participate if they bore responsibility for shoring up an ill-managed bank. Section Six of the Baltimore Plan stated: "The notes of insolvent banks should be redeemed by the Treasury of the United States, out of the 'Guarantee Fund' if it should be sufficient, and if not sufficient, then out of any money in the Treasury, the same to be reimbursed to the Treasury, out of the 'Guarantee Fund,' when replenished either from the assets of the failed banks or from the tax aforesaid." Each bank was to deposit in the Guarantee Fund 2 percent of the amount of the circulation received the first year. Thereafter, the tax would be at the rate of one-half of one percent per annum until the fund equaled 5 percent of the currency outstanding.

The report of the House committee (1894) considering the three plans concluded that requiring participating banks to share joint liability was not an "unreasonable requirement." The reason given was: "National banks enjoy valuable privileges and franchises. They owe something to the public, in consideration of the benefits they receive from legislation. If they are regardful of their own interests and the interests of the note holders there can be no loss to them nor to the note holders by reason of the requirement." Refusal to participate might be the most damaging criticism of an asset-based currency within a joint liability provision. This concern was probably exaggerated since the first line of defense against such a contingency was both the 5 percent safety fund and the 5 percent guaranty fund. In addition bank notes of failed banks constituted a first lien on all the banks' assets.

THE INDIANAPOLIS MONETARY COMMISSION

Renewed impetus for banking reform came four years later in 1898 with the recommendations of the Indianapolis Monetary Commission. The Baltimore Plan had been the work of bankers acting collectively through the ABA, but the idea for a national monetary conference originated with businessmen, not bankers. That business acting through trade associations could organize and mobilize public opinion gave a new twist to the movement for banking reform. An asset-based currency was the chief policy proposal of the Indianapolis Convention. Retirement of greenbacks and branch banking were also high on its list of priorities.

The idea for a national monetary conference on banking reform was first broached by H. H. Homer at a special meeting of the Board of Governors of the Indianapolis Board of Trade in November 1896. He stated that agitation among businessmen had reached a point where some response was necessary. And the response should have some central focus. To begin with, he thought letters should be sent to boards of trade in some sixteen cities in the central Midwest inviting members to a conference in Indianapolis on December 1 to consider a proposal for a national convention of boards of trade and other commercial organizations to create a commission to study the need for monetary and banking reform. Such a commission and its recommendations, he thought, should have a good chance of gaining the attention of Congress.

The preliminary conference representing twenty-six cities met as planned in Indianapolis and agreed to call a nonpartisan convention to meet in January 1897 comprised of around 250 businessmen chosen from boards of trade, chambers of commerce, and commercial clubs in cities of 8,000 or more in population; its purpose was to consider and to suggest legislation to place the currency system on a sound and permanent basis. Businessmen had a duty to participate. The session lasted two days, at which time an executive committee of fifteen members was selected. The executive committee should endeavor to obtain a special session of Congress to enact legislation calling for the appointment of a National Monetary Commission by the President and to report to Congress at the earliest possible date. Even this early it became clear that no such initiative could be expected from the politicized Congress.

If the attempt failed, the executive committee was authorized to select a commission of eleven members, one of whom was J. Lawrence Laughlin, professor of economics at the University of Chicago, and longtime advocate of banking reform. Two assistants were also named, former students of Laughlin, L. Carroll Root and H. Parker Willis. Its first meeting was held in September 1897. A list of more than thirty questions was drawn up to be sent to experts in the field. Twenty-six sessions of the commission were held with some regularity between October and December. At the final session a preliminary draft report was adopted by the commission, which was given to the public in January 1898. A few days later a bill was introduced in the U.S. House of Representatives by Jesse Overstreet of Indiana. The entire membership of the commission was reconvened on January 25 to hear the report of the Executive Committee.

The monetary commission had as its guide three fundamental considerations:

1. Maintenance of the gold standard
2. The ultimate retirement of all U.S. notes or greenbacks
3. The furnishing by the banking system of credit facilities to every portion of the country and a safe and elastic currency

The preliminary report identified major defects of the existing monetary and banking system including: (1) an inelastic national bank note issue which did not meet the needs of business; (2) a distribution of bank capital that failed to provide for the equalization of interest rates; and (3) inadequate provision for the redemption of government credit currency and confusion with the fiscal function of the Treasury as receivers and disbursers of revenue.

The national bank note issue was objectionable on three grounds: (1) it presupposed the continued issue of government bonds when national policy ought to be reduction of the national debt; (2) investment in bonds reduced the banks' funds available for loans; and (3) it did not respond to temporary changes in the demand for currency. The remedy was to base new issues on the banks' "readily convertible assets" which represented the "exchangeable wealth of the country." The alleged advantage would be its automaticity (p. 46): "Such a system would more perfectly than any other give the country a circulating medium, it would readily and quickly adjust itself from season to season to meet the needs of business of the country requiring bank notes for its convenient transactions." The danger of overissue would be minimal if redemption points were numerous. But an additional disincentive existed in the form of a tax at the rate of 2 percent per annum on the amount of notes in excess of 60 percent and not in excess of 80 percent of a participating bank's capital stock. The tax rate increased to 6 percent for amounts in excess of 80 percent of its capital.

Specific provision was made for the establishment of branch banks with the approval of the comptroller of the currency and the secretary of the treasury. The recommendation for branch banking was the commission's response to one of the three fundamental considerations governing its deliberations, that is, "the banking system should furnish credit facilities to every portion of the country . . ." No mention was made of branch banking as a remedy for the banking panic problem. The proposal was based solely on the alleged fact that deposits do not provide a desirable form of money for use in rural country districts. Note issue was restricted to national banks with minimal capital of $50,000. Banks of that capital size were presumably not fundamentally viable in small rural areas. And state banks without the note issue privilege were no solution to the problem. Branch banking would allegedly provide a better geographical distribution of bank capital and, as a desirable side effect, contribute to the equalization of interest rates among the various regions and districts of the United States.

The final report of the Indianapolis Monetary Commission contained in addition to the commission's recommendations a 600-page description of the U.S. monetary and banking system. It was prepared by Professor Laughlin and his two assistants and was not a joint effort of the eleven-member commission. He was aware of the shortcomings of his attempt, which he said "would have been much better done if it could have had the joint attention of the members of the Commission." There is no other report like it in American financial history. The Report of the National Monetary Commission in 1911 was only forty pages; however, there were twenty-three volumes of research studies that accompanied the report, each dealing with a specific subject. There was no attempt to provide a full description and analysis of the U.S. banking system. The Indianapolis Monetary Commission did not include in its terms of reference a survey of alternative remedies such as a central bank.

What influence, if any, did the commission exert on shaping the dialogue on banking reform? According to Livingston (1986, p. 118): "By the middle of 1898, the Monetary Commission had already established a broad ideological consensus within which the programmatic discussion of banking and monetary problem took shape." The Walker, Fowler, and McClary bills, he maintained, were based on the same principles espoused by the commission. Livingston (1986, p. 124) also attributed in part the passage of the Gold Standard Act of 1900 to the work of the commission: "strong pressure from the business community, through the movement initiated by the Indianapolis Monetary Commission of 1897–98, was the key to the passage of the gold standard legislation." Parity of all forms of U.S. money and the gold dollar and a division of function within the Treasury of the note issue and redemption had been top priorities of the commission. The IMC agendas of branch banking and an asset-based currency were less successful. The Executive Committee of the IMC continued to lobby Congress for banking reform in behalf of the Fowler bill in 1901 and 1902, with Homer as its chairman. He had been a member of the IMC and was the chief lobbyist for the bill.

The contributions to banking reform of the IMC were more political than economic. The case for an asset-based note issue was neither carefully argued nor specific enough in its application. The general principle was established, but no effort was made to meet the objections of critics, thereby weakened the persuasiveness of the proposal. Some advocates of an asset-based currency thought the privilege should be restricted to the larger, urban banks. Extending it to the smaller rural banks might encourage injudicious and imprudent issue of notes. Furthermore, the question of which assets should serve as a basis of the note issue was not specifically addressed.

The Indianapolis Monetary Commission was the first of its kind as a vehicle for banking reform. The initiative originated in the interior and not in New York or Washington. Moreover, it was national in scope and represented an attempt to enlist the cooperation of businessmen in the principal cities of the country. Although bankers as a group were not represented, there were prominent bankers in attendance; they contributed in part to meeting the convention's expenses. At least three distinguished economists were delegates: J. Lawrence Laughlin of the University of Chicago, Frank Taussig of Harvard, and Arthur T. Hadley of Yale. Henry Fowler, the leading spokesman for banking reform in the House of Representatives, was also a participant.

THE PRATT BILL: 1903

Departing from previous asset-based currency proposals, Senator Orville Pratt (1903) of New York, a close associate of Senator Aldrich, introduced a bill (S 2716) in January 1903 to incorporate national clearinghouses with the right to issue currency on the pledge of general assets. The power to issue an asset-based currency was lodged with the clearinghouse and not the individual banks. Since the clearinghouses had already assumed some panic-prevention responsibilities, the power to issue an asset-based currency would have strengthened their ability to cope with banking crises. And it would have been accomplished through collective action. The Pratt bill also gave legal status to clearinghouses and ensured that membership would not be restricted to a select number of banks determined solely by the clearinghouse itself. These associations were largely, though not entirely, restricted to clearinghouse associations with over $200 million of clearings. They could be formed with not less than five national banks in cities and towns with 6000 or more inhabitants. A provision to allow clearinghouses to issue currency was incorporated in the Aldrich-Vreeland Act in 1908.

Each association was to be governed by an elected board of directors. An elected loan committee was empowered to loan to participating banks on the basis of collateral that included commercial assets, promissory notes, bills of exchange, convertible bonds and stocks, and other securities not otherwise specified. Notes could be issued up to 75 percent of collateral value. And no bank could issue notes to exceed its capital stock. A fee of 1/50 of one percent was imposed on all clearing transactions. If the Pratt bill had passed it would have given legal status to clearinghouses and ensured that membership would not be restricted to a select number of banks as determined by each clearinghouse.

Legalizing clearinghouses was still being debated in the famous Money Trust Investigation in 1912 and 1913 but without success. The importance of the Pratt bill resides in the fact that a clearinghouse currency provision was included in the Aldrich-Vreeland Act and the issue of notes was not confined to periods of emergency. The bill received no further attention, having been quietly ignored.

THE NEW YORK CHAMBER OF COMMERCE

The movement for banking reform was advanced a stage further in 1906 when the New York Chamber of Commerce, an organization of influential businessmen, recommended the establishment of a U.S. central bank. However, an asset-based currency was not rejected outright. If the proposal for a central bank proved to be politically unacceptable, an asset-based currency would be a second-best solution, a tacit acknowledgment that such a currency was economically practical. The Chamber appointed a special five-man committee in March 1906 to inquire into the condition of the currency and suggest desirable changes. Members included Frank Vanderlip and Charles Conant. The secretary was an economist, Joseph French Johnson. The committee sought information from a variety of sources—clearing banks in principal cities, leading bankers in the United States, and heads of several European central banks. Conant himself made personal visits to several European central banks. The report of the committee was issued in October of the same year. It acknowledged the special responsibilities of the New York City banks, which should take the initiative in devising a program for banking reform acceptable to the rest of the country.

The report, unlike the Baltimore, Carlisle, and Eckels plans, did not recommend a phasing out of the national bank note circulation. Nor was there any objection to requiring the national banks to invest a certain proportion of their capital in government bonds as a condition of the issue of the new currency; they could still issue bond-secured currency up to the full amount of their capital. The report also identified what it regarded as the single major defect of the U.S. monetary system as seasonal inelasticity of the currency stock attributable to crop-moving demands and a bond-secured currency that was unresponsive. The result was a strong seasonal movement in interest rates, spikes at the peak of that demand and a collapse at the trough. It is inexplicable why so much attention was accorded seasonal demands and so little to panic-induced demands. Panic prevention was not a specific objective of the Chamber committee's deliberations.

The report suggested two remedies for an alleged defective and inelastic currency: a central bank of issue, the preferred remedy; and a second best asset-based currency. Although the report regarded a central bank as the best method for providing an elastic currency, details were absent about why a central bank currency issue was superior to that of an asset-based currency issued by individual banks. A central bank may have been desirable for other reasons, namely discount rate changes to restrain speculation as well as protect the nation's gold reserve. Moreover, it could also be used to smooth interest rates. The case for a central bank was neither well argued nor very persuasive.

The authors of the Chamber report revealed their reservations about the political feasibility of a central bank by devoting at least one-half of the document to a proposal for an asset-based currency. The amount of the new currency issued by individual national banks would be a fixed proportion of their capital stock. That the committee's attention was directed primarily at the problem of seasonality and not panic-induced demands is revealed by the estimates of the new currency needed during crop moving season, an amount equal to $150 million, or about 20 percent of the capital stock of all the national banks. On that basis, the report concluded that the proportion of the new issue to the capital stock should be between 25 and 35 percent. To ensure safety of the note issue, provision was made for adequate and convenient redemption facilities and a graduated tax imposed on the issue of notes, the tax increasing with an increase in the amount. A guaranty fund was also created from the proceeds of the graduated tax to redeem the notes of failed banks. The Chamber's recommendation for an asset-based currency, if a central bank proved politically infeasible, was a mere reflection of the Baltimore Plan and the proposals of the Indianapolis Monetary Commission. It also contained a provision heartily endorsing congressional action authorizing—through a voluntary association of banks, presumably—the clearinghouse to issue notes subject to certain limitations and a joint guarantee of the participating banks as long as it had been approved by the comptroller of the currency. The report also acknowledged the practical difficulties in getting the bankers to cooperate in establishing such a scheme. Nevertheless, as we shall see later, a similar provision was inserted in the Aldrich-Vreeland Act two years later.

The legacy of the Chamber's report was the planting of the seed that in the right political environment would grow into a U.S. style central bank. The report itself bungled the task of making the case for a central bank. The argument was insufficiently detailed to have demonstrated the clear superiority of a central bank to an asset-based currency.

THE ABA CURRENCY COMMISSION: 1906

Immediately following the submission of the final report of the Currency Committee of the New York Chamber of Commerce in October 1906, the ABA appointed a special commission to devise its own plan for banking reform. The earlier Baltimore Plan (1894) had not been commissioned by the ABA; it had originated with the Baltimore Clearing House and had been presented to the ABA for its consideration. Frank Vanderlip and Charles Conant, members of the Chamber committee, were invited to confer with the ABA commission. Vanderlip took part in its deliberations not as a member but as a consultant. The members of the fifteen-man commission included. A. B. Hepburn, chairman and president of Chase National Bank, James B. Forgan, president of the First National Bank of Chicago, Festus Wade, president of the Mercantile Trust Company of St. Louis, and Sol Wexler, vice-president, Whitney National Bank of New Orleans. Charles Fowler, chairman of the House Committee on Banking and Currency, was also in attendance and was prepared to introduce legislation resulting from the work of the commission. Some of the members of the commission had an interview with Senator Aldrich requesting information about how best to bring the commission's deliberations to the attention of Congress. In December 1906 House Bill 23017 was introduced by Fowler, reflecting the conclusions of the commission.

Like the Chamber's report, the commission identified the chief defect of the currency system as inelasticity. Currency demand depleted bank reserves, inducing a contraction of bank credit and deposits. The remedy did not take the form of devising a mechanism for supplying more reserves but, rather, of increasing the amount of bank notes each bank could create; bank notes not being part of the reserve, reserves would not be affected.

The principles which governed the commission's deliberations were stated, as follows:

1. An asset currency should be issued by national banks.
2. A bank note is essentially the same as a deposit payable on demand, resembling a cashier's check.
3. No action should be taken that might impair the market value of U.S. bonds.
4. The privilege of issuing notes should be extended to national banks that have been in existence for one year and whose surplus is equal to 20 percent of their capital.
5. These new credit notes should be taxed at a rate sufficient to provide a guarantee fund to redeem the notes of failed banks.
6. Reserve requirements should be the same for bank notes and for deposits.
7. Redemption of credit currency to ensure automaticity in the adjustment of the note currency to needs of business should be prompt (daily).

Each national bank would have the authority to issue bank notes with the following conditions:

(a) in an amount equal to 40 percent of its bond-secured currency
(b) not to exceed 25 percent of its capital
(c) subject to a tax of 2½ percent per annum on the average circulation
(d) an additional amount equal to 12½ percent of its capital
(e) subject to a 5 percent tax
(f) the total of credit and bond-secured currency not to exceed its capital.

Furthermore, government revenues above a reasonable working balance will be deposited in national banks without collateral requirements.

James Forgan (p. 163), a member of the commission, stated that the ABA plan was experimental and "existing conditions should be interfered with as little as possible and nothing of a radical nature recommended." He further stated that the commission was divided on whether to tax the new issue at a high or a low rate. The advocates of a high rate maintained that a high rate would impel the issuing bank to retire it as soon as conditions warranted. But he argued the issuing bank could neither call nor drive it in for redemption. Whether the note issue was redeemed or not depended entirely on the discretion of the note holder and not the issuing bank.

On the other hand, Forgan argued that a low-taxed note issue would adjust automatically to the needs of business. Banks have the incentive to redeem daily the notes of other banks for reserve money, the redemption taking place through the clearinghouse. The notes of any one bank will not continue to circulate any longer than the public's desire to hold them. Therefore, in his judgment, a redundant currency is impossible as demonstrated by experience in countries where they are in use, and thereby "emergencies avoided, panics prevented, and interest rates steadied and reduced." He thought the commission's plans were designed to meet both views. The new bank notes would ordinarily be paid out in exchange for a check, thereby providing a means of their getting into circulation. The balance sheet will show a reduction in deposit liabilities and an increase in demand note liabilities. Daily redemption lies at the heart of the plan to provide elasticity, and the commission requested that adequate redemption facilities be available, a fail-safe device for issuing an elastic currency.

No serious objections were raised at the time about how effective a tax on the circulating issue would be in ensuring early redemption. When the proposal called for a distinction between the regular and an emergency issue, a graduated rate would be applied to the emergency portion. The purpose of the tax was not only to ensure early redemption but to build a redemption fund and also to pay the Treasury's expenses for the note issue. Mints (1945) was skeptical that the imposition of a tax could influence the note issue. He concluded that most of the asset-based note issue proposals before 1913 "would in view of the then current rate of interest, either have had no effect on the value of the notes issued or have eliminated them altogether, for such proposals were usually for notes of 3 percent or less, or 6 percent or more" (p. 243). According to Mints, an increased demand for cash could be met by the banks in either of two different ways: calling of loans or the issue of notes. When equal, the bank would be indifferent between the two. Highly simplified, the indifference point would be reached when the rate of interest was equal to the tax rate on the note issue; that is, the bank's incentive to issue notes would vanish.

Mints did not think these considerations alone would determine the choice between loan contraction and note issue in the short run. But he did not specify what "short run" meant. A bank suffering a bank run would have no option but to issue notes. During a panic a spike in interest rates would move well above the tax rate and induce new issues. Nevertheless, the tax rate was low relative to the interest rate in the Baltimore, Carlisle, and Eckels plans, not in excess of one-half of one percent annually. The tax rate to replenish the safety fund only remained in effect as long as the fund was below 5 percent of the outstanding circulation. For these specific asset-based currency proposals, the tax rate on the note issue was not a deterrent to additional note issues.

THE COLUMBIA UNIVERSITY LECTURES

The shift of attention away from an asset-based currency to a central bank signaled by the New York Chamber of Commerce Report was reinforced by a series of nine lectures sponsored by Columbia University between 1907 and February 1908 undertaken at the initiative of Professor E. R. A. Seligman (1908). The occasion was the immediate aftermath of the 1907 banking panic; its purpose was to provide a public forum in order to sharpen the focus of the discussions on banking reform. The lecturers included some of the best banking talent in New York City. Frank Vanderlip and A. Barton Hepburn had both been active in the movement for banking reform. Paul Warburg was the most articulate spokesman for a U.S.-style central bank. Both Vanderlip and Hepburn endorsed a central bank as being preferable to an asset-based currency, which they regarded as second best.

The novelty of the lectures resided not so much in the advocacy of a central bank as in their contention that the chief defect of the banking system was decentralization, not the inelasticity of the note issue. Decentralization characterized the note issue among 6000 national banks; decentralization marked the banking reserve spread among central reserve city, reserve city, and country banks; it also included the absence of branch banking and the lack of any effective institutional mechanism for inducing cooperation and coordination of the individual banking units.

Although each national bank was required to hold reserves against its deposit liabilities, only a fraction was held in its own vault, the remainder being distributed among central reserve city and reserve city banks. As a result, the ultimate banking reserve came to be lodged among twelve or fifteen of the largest New York banks. The significance of the concentration, not decentralization, of the nation's banking reserve is presented in Wicker (2000, p. 117): "Of the approximately 60 members of the NYCH at least 15 held almost all of the bankers' balances of the New York banks." According to Sprague (1910, p. 233) seven of the banks in 1875 controlled 30 percent of all the resources of the New York banks, one-third of the loans and two-fifths of the cash reserve. By 1907 the degree of concentration of total reserves, loans, and cash reserves had increased substantially. Six banks holding the core of bankers' deposits controlled over 60 percent of the total reserves of the New York banks, 60 percent of the loans, and two-thirds of the cash reserves. Sprague (1910, p. 234) concluded, perhaps surprisingly, that "they would have yielded a banking power sufficient, it may be readily believed, for almost any emergency." The problem was not the decentralization of bank reserves, but their high concentration among a few select New York banks. During banking panics demands by interior banks fell uniquely among those select banks holding the majority of bankers' balances. The absence of any coordinated action by these banks led to the suspension of cash payments. Total reserves were adequate! The fault lay in the distribution of those balances. Knowing the likelihood of the suspension of cash payment by NYCH banks during banking crises, each national bank assumed responsibility for protecting and, if possible, adding to its reserve without regard to the effects of its own behavior on the behavior of other banks. The result was predictable, a mad scramble for the inflexible stock of bank reserves. Vanderlip (1908, p. 149) described the situation as follows: "Each institution stands alone, concerned for its own safety, and using every endeavor to pile up reserves without regard to what the effect may cost the financial situation at large." And Warburg (1908, p. 138) described it thus: "it forces each bank to look out for itself and to draw away the cash from the others, in order to increase the amount in its own vaults, thus aggravating the panic." It was hoarding by the banks, not hoarding of cash by the public, that was the true source of the trouble.

The remedy was clear at least to Dunbar (1907) and Sprague (1911): coordinated action by the NYCH banks to pool their reserves to meet the demands of the interior banks as it had done successfully in 1860 and 1861 and not so successfully in 1873 but rejected thereafter. Voluntary action by the NYCH banks to pool reserves was abandoned, and the memory of that experience faded despite the efforts of Dunbar and Sprague to keep it alive.

Vanderlip attributed the inept U.S. currency system to serious legal constraints in the form of laws restricting the diffusion of branch banking and the issue of bank notes tied to the purchase of U.S. government securities. He thought the 1907 panic could be "laid at the door of improper and inadequate legislation." Vanderlip recognized that "there is profound political prejudice against both of these ideas," but he found no sound foundations for these prejudices and thought they could be overcome if sufficient resources were allocated for an intensive campaign to educate the public on the necessity of banking reform.

In their lectures Vanderlip, Hepburn, and Warburg acknowledged the ideal currency system was a European style central bank. Each pointed to the successful note issuance by the Bank of England, the Bank of France, and the Reichsbank, contrasted with the unproven, decentralized asset-based currency here. However, in the event the idea of a central bank was politically unacceptable, Vanderlip and Hepburn were prepared to accept less. Vanderlip (1908, p.17) even considered the possibility of an expansion of the powers of the clearinghouse, which might be "more in harmony with the preset political ideas than will either branch banking or a central bank."

Although Hepburn had endorsed an asset-based currency plan devised by the ABA commission, he judged a central bank to be superior both from a scientific and historical standpoint. The experience of both Germany and England was sufficient grounds for preferring a central bank. There were additional advantages—the smoothing of interest rates and the transfer of the Treasury's monetary responsibilities. Both Vanderlip and Hepburn thought that the public's opposition to a central bank had been exaggerated, and with an energetic plan to educate public opinion, that opposition might be overcome.

Even though Warburg's ideal solution for the U.S. currency problems was a European style central bank, he did not think that it was economically feasible in the absence of a discount market and a suitable financial instrument for trading in that market. The American promissory note was not tradable. European bills usually had two endorsements, and few American bills qualified. Warburg rejected asset-based currency proposals. He offered a transitory solution in the form of a central clearinghouse with the power to issue notes against clearinghouse certificates, calling it the "best solution for the time being." The central clearinghouse would have a capital of its own, limited dividend payments, and surpluses accruing to the government— features eventually embodied in the Aldrich bill (1911). The alleged advantages of such a scheme were centralization of the note issue to accommodate commerce and industry and the fact that it would not disturb the existing banking structure. He recognized that a large gap existed between the ideal and what was politically feasible. Any immediate attempt would be futile.

The Columbia lectures were a reflection of the state of opinion of some influential New York bankers on the question of banking reform immediately prior to the passage of the Aldrich-Vreeland bill in 1908. The ideal solution was a central bank and branch banking. However, with an eye to pending legislation, the ideal was separated from the politically feasible. An asset-based currency still held the national spotlight either in the form of note issue by the more than 6000 national banks or some form of central clearinghouse, a quasi central bank with the power to issue emergency notes. The former prevailed with the passage of Aldrich-Vreeland in May 1908. The Aldrich-Vreeland Act was the culmination of fourteen years of deliberations about an asset-based currency as the cornerstone of banking reform. It warrants a separate chapter as the transition phase to the creation of a central bank. Due to expire in 1914, Aldrich-Vreeland was never regarded as anything more than a temporary measure to tidy things over until the National Monetary Commission could come up with a more permanent solution. As a panic-preventive device it was superior to both the Aldrich and the Glass-Owen bills.

This chapter has traced the history of asset-based currency proposals beginning with the Baltimore Plan in 1894 through the ABA Currency Commission Report in 1906. Up to that time the debate had focused solely on the various asset-based currency proposals, their strengths and their weaknesses. The second stage of the Great Debate on banking reform commenced in 1906 with the simultaneous report of the New York Chamber of Commerce. Although the Chamber report proposed a central bank, it concluded that if a central bank proved to be politically unacceptable, an asset-based currency would be a second best solution. More than one-half of the report was devoted to an asset-based currency. The narrative ends with the Columbia University Lectures in 1907 and 1908 devoted entirely to the establishment of a central bank. A separate chapter will describe how the debate about the various asset-based currency proposals was finally resolved with the passage of the Aldrich-Vreeland Act in 1908. Thereafter, proposals for a central bank monopolized all further discussions of banking reform.

What the asset-based currency proposals had in common were these goals:

1. Note issue being a function of banks, not the government
2. The issue of an asset-based currency, mainly commercial paper, with safety and guaranty features
3. The elimination of the bond-secured national bank notes
4. The retirement of U.S. greenbacks.

Pratt and the New York Chamber of Commerce endorsed the issue of an asset-based currency through the collective action of the clearinghouse associations, which, as we shall see in the next chapter, was incorporated in the Aldrich-Vreeland Act. What is somewhat surprising is the absence of panic-prevention as a specific objective of banking reform.

CHAPTER FOUR

The Aldrich-Vreeland Act

In the aftermath of the 1907 banking panic Congress began serious consideration of what legislative action might be necessary to prevent a repetition of such banking crises in the future. Its response was dictated by political sentiment as interpreted by Republican party leaders who reasoned that they would be held responsible in a presidential election year if the Congress failed to act. There was no dearth of proposals from which to choose. Edward Vreeland, Henry Fowler, and James McKinney had introduced bills in the House of Representatives. But neither the Fowler nor the McKinney bills could gain widespread House support. Fowler (1906), who was chairman of the House Banking and Currency Committee, reintroduced a bill he had originally submitted in1906. Between 1906 and 1908 his bill had lost the support of the ABA, although the association approved of his specific proposal to issue an asset-based currency. The bill also contained additional provisions for the guaranty of deposits and a guaranty fund to ensure the notes of failed banks, both of which the ABA disapproved of. It also called for the abolition of the independent treasury system and the eventual retirement of greenbacks, which turned out to be more than the House could digest.

Nelson Aldrich, chairman of the Senate Finance Committee, made his unsuccessful debut in the banking reform debate. He favored an emergency currency bill with the least possible departures from existing practice. As a bond-secured currency advocate, he simply extended the list of eligible securities that could serve as a basis for an emergency circulation to include obligations of state and local governments as well as railroad mortgage bonds. At this juncture he was resolutely opposed to an asset-based currency if it included commercial paper. Bank notes could be issued up to 75 percent of their market value. A tax of one-half of one percent was levied on notes secured by U.S. bonds bearing less than 2 percent interest and one percent on all other securities. The bill also required country banks to hold in their vaults at least two-thirds of the 15 percent reserve requirement. Unexpectedly strong opposition developed to the inclusion of railroad bonds, which were mostly held by large New York banks with lesser amounts held in the interior. The eligibility of railroad bonds was regarded as an exclusive boon to New York bankers at the expense of banks in the rest of the country. Aldrich was forced to remove railroad bonds from the final version of the bill and the reserve provision as well. With this change it was approved by the Senate but ran into trouble in the House.

Unwilling to pass the Aldrich bill and finding the Fowler bill objectionable, Edward Vreeland introduced a substitute measure in May 1908. The Vreeland bill authorized the creation of a national clearinghouse association made up of not less than ten banks with an aggregate surplus of at least $5 million. Each national bank could issue notes on any security including commercial paper provided the bank had outstanding bank notes secured by U.S. bonds of not less than 40 percent of its capital and limited in amount to 75 percent of the cash value of the securities. The notes constituted a lien on all the assets of the participating banks. The House passed the Vreeland bill by a large majority, but it turned out to be unacceptable to the Senate. The impasse was resolved by conference committee, which managed to iron out the differences by embodying the main provisions of both bills, that is, an asset- and a bond-secured currency.

The view prevailed in Congress that permanent banking reform would not be possible during the 1908 session; the votes were simply not there. Although opposition was strong, a stopgap measure was still thought desirable. The Aldrich-Vreeland Act scheduled to expire at the end of June 1914 was clearly recognized to be a temporary measure to bridge the gap until more permanent legislation could be adopted. Aldrich's Senate bill had provided for the appointment of a National Monetary Commission "to inquire into and report to Congress at the earliest date possible, what changes were necessary or desirable in the monetary system of the United States or in the laws relating to banking and currency . . ." The idea of a National Monetary Commission was not new. It had been suggested to the House Banking and Currency Committee as early as June 1884. During the House hearings on the Aldrich bill, Victor Morawetz (1908, pp. 28 and 42) and James Forgan (1908, p. 236) recommended the appointment of a commission to study banking reform. Charles N. Fowler (1906) and George F. Burgess (1908) introduced bills in the House of Representatives that included such a provision.

Aldrich-Vreeland embodied what was thought to be politically feasible as of May 8, 1908. Aldrich had dismissed any proposal for a central bank as immature and politically infeasible. The debates between the advocates of a bond-secured and an asset-based currency had ended in the sense that both could serve as the basis for the issue of an emergency currency. The real significance of the act resided in the inclusion of commercial paper. The authority to issue credit currency did not reside solely with the individual bank. Securities to be used had to be approved by a local currency association. The significance of the Aldrich-Vreeland bill has not always been appreciated. It effectively put an end to the debate over asset-based currency proposals by settling on one. And more importantly, Aldrich-Vreeland provided a viable solution to the banking panic problem. Had the elimination of banking panics been the sole incentive for establishment of a central bank, Aldrich-Vreeland rendered a central bank redundant. Nevertheless, the debate on permanent banking reform continued with the appointment of the National Monetary Commission.

THE 1914 BANKING PANIC

The Aldrich-Vreeland Act successfully forestalled an incipient banking panic in August 1914 at the outset of World War I. The banking crisis in August 1914 bears a closer resemblance to the 1861 crisis than it does to all the other banking disturbances of the National Banking Era. Both had their origins in the outbreak of war, the Civil War in 1861 and World War I in 1914. In the earlier crisis Southerners attempted to liquidate assets held in the North in 1861, and foreign investors attempted to dispose of American securities at fire-sale prices, thereby disrupting the stock and the foreign exchange markets. The banking crisis in 1861 did not result in a banking panic because the NYCH banks agreed to the pooling of their reserves. In 1914 a panic was forestalled by the issue of emergency currency authorized by the amended Aldrich-Vreeland Act and the issue of clearinghouse loan certificates by NYCH banks. Banking panics were successfully prevented in both war-related episodes. Part of the success can probably be attributed to the willingness of the banks to subordinate their selfish interests to the general good of the nation, especially when its security was threatened. We know the cooperative spirit did not extend into the post–Civil War period. It is useless to speculate whether the issue of an emergency currency would have prevented the banking panics of the Great Depression, but we do know that it could not have been worse than the policies that actually were pursued by Fed policymakers.

The 1914 crisis had the immediate effect of closing both the stock and foreign exchange markets. The cash reserves of the NYCH banks and trust companies fell by $56 million for the week ending July 31, and $44 million of gold was withdrawn for export. Collateral for bank loans could not be liquidated, thereby increasing the pressure on the banks to extend loan accommodation. The response to the incipient banking crisis was not slow in coming. The secretary of the treasury announced on August 3 that he was prepared to immediately approve the issue of $100 million of currency notes by national banks in New York City under the terms spelled out in the Aldrich-Vreeland Act, and to authorize their issue by national banks in the rest of the country. Furthermore, as in previous panics, the NYCH responded on August 3 by authorizing the issue of clearinghouse loan certificates. Between August 3 and October 15, the NYCH issued $125 million of clearinghouse loan certificates. The issues were fully cancelled by the end of November, 118 days after the initial issue. This compares favorably with a duration of 154 days in 1907 and approximately the same in 1893. Loan certificates were issued by clearinghouses in New York, Chicago, St. Louis, New Orleans, Philadelphia, and Boston, as well as a few other cities.

The highly volatile situation in New York was quickly defused. Both the issue of emergency currency and clearinghouse certificates enabled the New York banks to conserve their reserves and thereby make possible a liberal expansion of bank loans, the sine qua non for restoring banking confidence. These two measures restored stability to the money market; there were no spikes in interest rates and—most important of all—no suspension of cash payments. During August $200 million of Aldrich-Vreeland notes were issued, and by the end of October that sum had reached over $350 million. After the crisis had subsided, their retirement was fairly rapid.

The Aldrich-Vreeland Act had been scheduled to expire at the end of June 1914, but a provision in the original Federal Reserve Act extended its life for another year and reduced the tax rate on new note issues from 5 to 3 percent for the first three months thereafter, increasing one-half percent a month until a maximum of 6 percent was reached. Although the Federal Reserve Act was passed in December 1913, the Reserve Banks did not open until November 1914. To meet the August crisis it was necessary to invoke the provisions of the Aldrich-Vreeland Act. Congress amended the act during the first week in August to eliminate the requirement that no bank could issue emergency notes if it had already issued bond-secured currency up to 40 percent of its capital. Without the amendment, the banks' incentive to issue new currency would have been seriously compromised.

Aldrich-Vreeland allowed national banks to issue emergency currency when they were organized into currency associations with no less than ten participants with a minimum capital of $5 million. Only 21 associations with 325 banks had been organized in the five years since the passage of the Aldrich-Vreeland Act. But during the two months of August and September 1914 the number of associations doubled to 44 with 2,102 participating banks representing about 70 percent of the combined capital and surplus of all national banks. Currency was issued by 41 of the 44 associations and approximately 57 percent of the member banks. The New England and southern states had the highest proportion of banks issuing currency to the total number of participating banks, 45 and 42 percent respectively. The eastern states were next with 24 percent; three regions had proportions of less than 10 percent. Table 1 (pp. 48–49) lists all of the currency associations and their authorized currency issues. The number of banks in each currency association varied widely from a low of 10 in central New York State to a high of 281 in Dallas, which included many banks in contiguous areas. Of the $375 million of currency authorized, approximately 60 percent originated in four cities: New York (40%), Philadelphia (4%), Boston (8%), and Chicago (7%), with the remainder being distributed over the country as a whole. The currency association in Cincinnati, for example, issued a little less than $9.4 million in emergency notes, which represented less than 20 percent of the authorized amount. Thirty-three of the issuing banks were located in 16 cities in Ohio, 8 banks in 6 cities of Kentucky, and 3 banks in 2 cities in West Virginia. The Boston currency association issued $29 million of currency, which represented 43 percent of the authorized amount. There were 70 participating banks, 11 in Boston and 59 in Massachusetts. The Louisville currency association issued approximately $8 million in notes, of which $4.6 million was issued by 23 banks in Kentucky, $3 million by 25 banks in Tennessee, and $15,000 by 2 banks in Indiana. Notes were not issued in only nine small states: Maine, Vermont, Rhode Island, South Dakota, Wyoming, Utah, Nevada, and North and South Dakota. Table 1 reveals how geographically dispersed was the bankers' response to the provisions of the Aldrich-Vreeland Act. Of the $375 million of currency issued, 51 percent was secured by commercial paper, 14 percent by state and municipal bonds, 28 percent by miscellaneous securities, and one-half percent by warehouse receipts. The newly issued notes were used both for payments to depositors and payments between banks. They even tended to be used instead of clearinghouse certificates as payment between banks since the tax on the increased note issue was 3 percent compared with a rate of 6 percent on clearinghouse certificates.

By issuing an asset currency, the banks as anticipated conserved their reserves and were more than able to meet domestic requirements, though they were extremely reluctant to use their reserves to meet foreign demands. Between June 30 and September 12, loans and investments of all national banks increased by $207 million. Contrasted with previous banking crises, the banks did not attempt to strengthen themselves by loan contraction. Sprague (1915, p. 519) concluded: "Thanks to the emergency notes, the banks maintained payments without restrictions on their dealings both with the public and between themselves." The Aldrich-Vreeland Act was far more successful as a panic-preventive measure than anyone could have anticipated at the time of its passage. Had the level of confidence in its success been higher, there would have been no need for a national monetary commission to study and make recommendations for permanent banking reform. So successful was the use of A-V emergency notes that Sprague (1914, p. 184) stated: "It is a safe conclusion that, if similar notes had been available in former crises, the results would be equally satisfactory. The dislocation of the domestic exchanges, the premium on currency, and the partial breakdown of the check machinery of the country would have been avoided." Nevertheless, the original Aldrich-Vreeland Act contained provisions that could have restricted participation. As amended by the Federal Reserve Act and by amendments in August 1914 these provisions were eliminated. The tax on emergency currency issued was reduced, and the provision restricting new issues by those banks that had bond-secured currency up to 40 percent of their capital and surplus was also removed.

The banks successfully avoided the cessation of cash payments. The issue of A-V notes also safeguarded the reserves of the banks, enabling them to supply additional loans, unlike in previous banking panics. Rates were maintained within reasonable bounds. According to Sprague (1915, p. 521), "this was the first crisis in the United States in which the situation was handled in the only proper fashion, that is, by means of loan expansion." Laughlin (1920, p. 128) had worried that an asset-based currency as provided for by the Aldrich-Vreeland Act was not a solution to the banking panic problem because it ignored the necessity for liberal loan expansion which, he thought, could only be resolved by establishing a mechanism for the creation of reserves. The 1914 episode revealed that Laughlin's fears were unfounded. The issue of emergency currency conserved the reserves of the banks, thereby freeing them for loan expansion.

An early stage of the Great Debate on banking reform ended inconclusively with the passage of the Aldrich-Vreeland Act. Had the experience of the 1914 banking crisis been available earlier, the question of panic prevention would have been resolved without the necessity for a central bank. The earlier advocates for banking reform had been correct. An asset-based currency was a more effective substitute for a central bank if and only if panic prevention were the sole objective of banking reform. Whereas

Table 1

National currency associations: their membership, capital, surplus, and authorized issues of "additional circulation" on Oct. 31, 1914

Association	Number of Banks	Capital	Surplus	Authorized Issues of Additional Circulation
Washington, DC	12	$6,752,000	$5,128,000	$637,000
City of New York	40	144,750,000	126,835,000	144,965,000
City of Philadelphia	65	31,340,000	50,102,000	14,323,750
State of Louisiana (New Orleans)	45	9,635,000	6,337,865	4,814,000
City of Boston	70	39,460,000	28,474,000	28,674,500
Georgia (Atlanta)	92	14,920,000	9,865,500	6,737,400
City of Chicago	12	43,100,000	26,690,000	27,070,000
St. Louis	41	25,330,000	11,813,000	10,582,500
The Twin Cities (St. Paul, Minn.)	35	18,475,000	13,660,000	12,727,500
City of Detroit	20	9,950,000	5,665,000	2,414,000
Albany, Rensselaer, and Schenectady Counties (Albany)	32	6,050,000	5,932,000	4,704,000
Kansas City and St. Joseph, MO	42	11,790,000	6,113,000	5,319,250
City of Baltimore	22	11,495,710	8,267,210	7,922,000
Cincinnati, OH	99	28,960,000	16,018,000	9,361,000
Dallas, TX	286	25,260,000	13,844,200	10,429,050
Alabama (Montgomery)	75	9,865,000	6,234,800	4,088,550
Denver, Colorado Springs, and Pueblo	16	4,900,000	4,942,500	1,395,000
Los Angeles, CA	71	11,860,000	5,057,000	3,701,000
Louisville, KY	69	16,175,000	7,618,100	6,874,900
San Francisco, CA	25	33,125,000	19,460,000	8,565,000
Pittsburgh, PA	37	32,700,000	25,463,000	10,507,000
Cleveland, OH	26	16,210,000	8,886,500	8,123,000
Indianapolis, IN	29	10,960,000	5,047,500	419,500
Richmond, VA	50	12,970,000	9,174,500	6,139,600
Buffalo of Western New York	39	10,193,000	8,497,500	5,961,000
Raleigh, NC	60	7,945,000	3,276,750	3,415,450
Des Moines, IA	163	14,025,000	6,815,333	2,235,875
Omaha	18	6,700,000	4,021,000	1,833,000

continued

Table 1 Continued

Association	Number of Banks	Capital	Authorized Issues of Additional Surplus	Circulation
Seattle, WA	12	6,850,000	2,315,000	490,000
Peoria, IL	12	3,150,000	2,000,000	172,000
Columbia, SC	48	7,160,000	2,575,800	2,570,980
Scranton, PA	12	4,235,000	6,275,000	300,000
Fort Worth, TX	153	12,705,000	6,421,083	4,507,500
Houston, TX	41	7,850,000	3,666,950	2,456,950
Rochester, NY	23	3,950,000	3,557,700	831,000
Utica, NY	12	4,225,000	3,275,000	—
City of Milwaukee	21	8,865,000	4,473,000	4,006,000
Providence, RI	12	5,420,000	4,390,000	—
Portland, OR	17	6,875,000	3,240,000	1,976,000
New Haven, CT	43	15,744,200	9,886,800	1,162,000
San Antonio, TX	37	4,720,000	2,370,500	640,000
Jacksonville, FL	30	4,280,000	1,955,000	1,342,500
Manchester, NH	28	3,495,000	2,865,000	305,000
Syracuse, NY	10	3,255,000	1,770,000	—
Totals	2,102	687,494,910	510,276,091	374,680,715

Source: Report of the Comptroller of the Currency. December 7, 1914. Government Printing Office. Washington, 1915, p. 60.

Aldrich-Vreeland was directed solely at panic prevention, the establishment of a central bank introduced multiple objectives. That an asset-based currency as provided for in the Aldrich-Vreeland Act could and did forestall an incipient banking panic was clearly and convincingly demonstrated in August 1914. However, the evidence of its feasibility came too late, much too late to have been a decisive factor in the debate on a U.S. style central bank.

THE NATIONAL MONETARY COMMISSION

Unwilling to tackle the problem of permanent banking reform, the Congress inserted a provision in the Aldrich-Vreeland Act creating a National Monetary Commission made up of nine members of the House of Representatives and nine senators, with Nelson Aldrich as its chairman.

By removing congressional committee deliberation from its traditional role, Congress believed it would be less partisan and thereby expedite a consensus for permanent banking reform. The idea for such a monetary commission was not new. As mentioned previously, the House Banking and Currency Committee had made such a suggestion as early as June 1884. During the hearings on the Aldrich bill in 1908 Victor Morawetz (1908, pp. 26, 42) and James Forgan (1908, p. 236) both recommended the appointment of an independent commission to study banking reform. The phrase "independent commission" was ambiguous. Whether that included members of Congress or outside experts was not specified.

According to Andrew (Gray, 1971, pp. 71–73) the National Monetary Commission was a "one-man show" completely dominated by Senator Aldrich, who thought this was his one opportunity for enduring fame. The commission was merely window dressing for Aldrich's initiatives. He expected and received little help from the congressional appointees, whose knowledge of money and banking was confined to what Andrew had tried to teach them on the way over to Europe in the summer of 1908. Aldrich himself was not a student of banking. To rectify his knowledge gap he surrounded himself with a carefully chosen few "banker consultants," two New York bankers, Henry Davison, a J.P. Morgan partner, and Frank Vanderlip, vice-president of National City Bank (the largest bank in New York), and George Reynolds of Continental Bank of Chicago and president of the ABA. Aldrich also worked closely with Andrew, who was on leave from the economics department at Harvard.

No one in 1908 could have predicted the outcome of the commission's deliberations. Aldrich himself had been opposed to a central bank whose time had not arrived. Although the bankers were not fully satisfied with the Aldrich-Vreeland Act, they had not switched their allegiance to a U.S. style central bank. Opinion favoring a central bank was largely confined to a few very articulate New York bankers. One of the first tasks of the commission during the summer of 1908 was to visit the various European capitols and to conduct interviews with central bank officials and distinguished bankers. Davison played a leading role in arranging these meetings and, as a Morgan partner, carried enough clout to ensure ready compliance with the commission's request for interviews and information.

The commission made little progress in 1909. Aldrich, according to McCulley (1992, p. 226) was distracted by the debates on the tariff bill that were focused on a reduction in rates. He was the recognized expert on tariffs in the U.S. Senate. Understandably, his attention was deflected from banking reform. Most of the next year was not much better. Aldrich spent his time informing a broader public about the work of the commission and the necessity for banking reform. There is little evidence that the commission was making much progress. However, the tempo accelerated towards the end of the year when Aldrich arranged a clandestine meeting of his New York banker associates at Jekyll Island off the coast of Georgia to prepare a report outlining the main provisions of a banking reform bill. The political horizon became clouded in anticipation of the midterm elections. The Democrats gained control of the House of Representatives for the first time since 1894. Aldrich's grip on the Republican party was weakened as a result of rising insurgency among southern and western party members, who were more inclined to follow Roosevelt and the progressives than Aldrich and his conservative associates.

CHAPTER FIVE

JEKYLL ISLAND AND THE ALDRICH BILL

Two and one-half years had passed and the National Monetary Commission had still not made its report to Congress. Henry Davison, a Morgan partner and consultant to the commission, suggested to Aldrich that a few trusted advisers form a working party for the purpose of drafting a banking reform bill that could be presented to Congress as the result of the work of the National Monetary Commission. The ideal location, he thought, was a remote private island off the southeastern coast of Georgia, which J. P. Morgan and other wealthy moguls used as a hunting and recreation retreat. According to Davison's biographer, Thomas Lamont (1933, p. 97), Aldrich agreed and asked Davison to select the participants; they were sworn to secrecy by Aldrich and were to travel incognito to avoid contact with the press. Stephenson (1930, p. 376) relates that when the party arrived at Brunswick, Georgia, the station master greeted them with a surprising remark: "We know who you are and reporters are waiting outside." Davison is reported to have said "Come out, old man, I will tell you a story . . ." We do not know what Davison told the station master, but when he returned smiling, he said "they won't give us away." The reporters disappeared and no more was heard of the Jekyll Island rendezvous until it was revealed by Stephenson in his biography of Nelson Aldrich published in 1930.

The participants included Aldrich, his personal secretary Arthur Shelton, Henry Davison, Frank Vanderlip, Paul Warburg, and A. Piatt Andrew. Vanderlip (1935, p. 213) in his memoirs claimed that a seventh person was also present, Benjamin Strong, vice-president of Bankers Trust and future governor of the Federal Reserve Bank of New York: "Those who had been asked to go were Henry Davison, Paul Warburg, Benjamin

Strong and myself. From Washington came A. Piatt Andrew who was then Assistant Secretary of the Treasury." There is no reference to a Jekyll Island meeting in Chandler's (1952) biography of Strong. Nor does Stephenson (1930, p. 375) identify Strong as a participant. In an oral interview Andrew granted Everett Case he failed to mention Strong as a member of the working party: "The first rough draft of a bill was actually evolved at the famous meeting at Jekyll Island, attended by Mr. Davison, Mr. Warburg, and Mr. Vanderlip, as well as the Senator, his secretary and myself. This was in the Winter of 1909 [*sic*], I think, and the meeting was kept secret lest it be charged that Wall Street was dictating the bill." In a private memorandum prepared for Davison's biography by Thomas Lamont (1933, p. 98), Paul Warburg wrote:

> The small party, consisting of Senator Aldrich, Mr. Shelton, secretary, and Professor A. Piatt Andrew, special assistant to the Monetary Commission, Davison, Frank A. Vanderlip, and myself, set out on its trip to Jekyl [*sic*] Island in November, 1910. It spent a week in complete seclusion and privacy, and it developed and formulated then and there the first draft of what later became known as the Aldrich bill.

The evidence seems to point clearly in the direction that Strong was not at Jekyll Island. But it leaves unexplained Vanderlip's lapse of memory. Neither Vanderlip nor Warburg was associated with the National Monetary Commission. Davison had acted as a special consultant to Aldrich on banking matters and had accompanied the commission on its trip to Europe in the summer of 1908. And Andrew had been a special assistant to the commission, but at the time of Jekyll Island he was assistant secretary of the treasury. There is no record of the proceedings of the Jekyll Island meeting. Aldrich's private secretary, who was also present, took stenographic minutes, but they were either lost or destroyed. Aldrich's request for absolute secrecy was honored. Even after the veil of secrecy was lifted with the publication of Stephenson's biography of Aldrich, we still do not know what each of the participants contributed, with the possible single exception of Warburg, who had published a draft of a central bank proposal. Vanderlip, as quoted by Stephenson (1930, p. 484), wrote many years later: "none of us knew certainly what Mr. Aldrich wanted in the way of a new banking bill. As a matter of fact Mr. Aldrich knew about as little of what he wanted as we did." But that uncertainty did not extend to the necessity for a central bank. As we have seen, Aldrich had become a convert after the visit of the commission to Europe in the summer of 1908. Vanderlip and Warburg were already on record as favoring a central bank that could issue an asset-based currency. What the working party had to decide was: What kind of central bank?

The Jekyll Island meeting was remarkable for a number of reasons: not only was the public not informed about such a meeting but also members of the Monetary Commission remained in the dark as well; Andrew was serving as assistant secretary of the treasury, and his participation was unknown to Secretary of the Treasury Franklin C. MacVeigh. The idea that an official of the Taft administration was directly involved in the drafting of a banking reform bill without knowledge of the administration was probably without precedent. Even more anomalous was the fact that three Wall Street bankers were enlisted to draft a banking reform bill! Had their presence become known, Aldrich's credibility would have suffered a serious setback. Aldrich certainly understood the political risk he was taking in convening a secret meeting of Wall Street bankers. Only Aldrich's conceit and contempt for the contribution of the members of the commission could have induced him to undertake such a daring and risky adventure. Although the participants with the exception of Andrew were well known in their day, time has not been kind to any of them. To remove some of this ignorance, I provide brief sketches of each member of the group, beginning with its leader Senator Aldrich.

NELSON ALDRICH

Agitation for banking reform in the United States was almost continuous in this country after 1894. But the voices for reform rarely attained national attention. Proposals multiplied for an asset-based currency to replace the bond-secured currency mandated by the National Banking Act. Branch banking and deposit insurance were also considered as possible solutions to the banking panic problem. Numerous bills were introduced into Congress but without gaining congressional approval. Leadership was lacking. The tariff question preempted banking reform considerations, and there had been no serious banking panic since 1893. The archconservative leader of the Republicans, Senator Nelson Aldrich, according to his biographer Nathaniel Stephenson (1930, p. 223), preferred to "let sleeping dogs lie." The sleeping dogs could no longer lie after the panic of 1907, which was a catalyst for banking reform. Thereafter, the pace of reform quickened, leading ultimately to the passage of the Federal Reserve Act.

The key player in the movement for banking reform was Nelson Aldrich, the six-term senator from Rhode Island (figure 1). His contributions to the establishment of the Federal Reserve System were deliberate-

Figure 1 Nelson W. Aldrich

ly obscured by Carter Glass (1927, pp. 239–44) and Parker Willis (1923, p. 523), who took great pains to denigrate his influence. To admit that Aldrich might have influenced the Glass-Owen bill would be to repudiate the plank in the Democratic platform that was opposed to a central bank and the Aldrich bill.

Aldrich was well qualified for the dauntless task before him. His experience in the Senate was unrivaled. No other Republican had dared challenge his leadership. Tariff legislation had been his chief claim to political and national recognition. Although a staunch conservative with a Hamiltonian conception of a strong central government, he had a firm grasp of the persuasive and other parliamentary skills for moving legislation successfully through Congress.

Before 1903, most of his attention was directed at tariff legislation and the protection of manufacturing interests. However, as early as 1903, Aldrich, according to Stephenson (1930, p. 216), "buckled down to the task of learning about the theories of banking and currency." He had drafted a banking bill which gave the secretary of the treasury the power to use obligations other than those of the federal government as security for deposits of public money. But it went nowhere. However, as a consequence of his lack of success, he appointed a subcommittee of the Finance Committee to consider the necessity for banking legislation. The subcommittee held one meeting. Nothing came of it except to turn Aldrich's interests in a new direction.

We hear no more from Aldrich about banking reform until the aftermath of the 1907 banking panic. He introduced a bill in the Senate to provide an emergency currency. The measure was intended only as an interim gesture until a more permanent solution could be worked out. The Aldrich-Vreeland Act (1908) created the National Monetary Commission—nine members of the Senate and nine members of the House with Senator Aldrich as Chairman—to study monetary and banking conditions both in the United States and abroad with a view to serving as a basis for discussion and fruitful legislation.

His senatorial experience was as much a weakness as it was a strength. It gave him a firm grip on senatorial power that was unrivaled, and with the sense of power a certain arrogance and aloofness and seeming indifference to the views of most of his colleagues in Congress. Aldrich was in the habit of having things his own way without having to defer to the judgment of others. His initiatives were rarely blocked, but it was becoming increasingly difficult to bring them to fruition.

Piatt Andrew (Gray, 1971, p. 73) recalled that the Monetary Commission was a "one man show completely dominated by Senator Aldrich who thought this was his one opportunity for enduring fame." Aldrich expected little help from commission members, all of whom according to Andrew "he knew he could control." He simply wanted to keep them happy until the bill was forthcoming and then get their approval. Nor did he expect much help from his colleagues in the Senate. He sought advice from bankers, financial writers, and economists.

In addition to the congressional members of the commission, Aldrich asked Henry Davison, a Morgan partner, to be a special consultant on U.S. banking practice, as well as George Reynolds, president of Continental Illinois Bank in Chicago. A. Piatt Andrew, an assistant professor, was enlisted with the aid of President Eliot of Harvard to be chief economist. These four were entrusted with the real work of the commission.

One of the first tasks of the commission during the summer of 1908 was to visit various European capitols and to conduct interviews with central bank officials and distinguished bankers. The stenographic minutes of these meetings were published among the twenty scholarly volumes for the commission. Davison played an important role in arranging these meetings, as stated previously.

Aldrich had partially overcome his strong commitment to a bond-secured currency when he agreed to sponsor an asset-based currency proposal in the Aldrich-Vreeland Act in 1908. But he still had to be persuaded of the desirability of a central bank. The commission's European trip convinced Aldrich of the necessity for a central bank and removed whatever doubts still existed about the desirability of an asset-based currency that would expand and contract to meet the needs of business. German banking practice was responsible for his conversion. Representative Theodore Burton of Ohio, a commission member, dated Aldrich's conversion to that visit.

Returning home from the foreign trip, he had formulated two of the cornerstones of fundamental banking reform: a central bank (on the order of the Reichsbank), and an asset-based currency—a necessary instrument to provide an elastic currency. The technical details of establishing a central bank and an asset-based currency he left to be worked out later.

As the time approached when the commission would have to report to Congress, Davison as we have seen suggested to Aldrich that a secret meeting be held at Jekyll Island with a view to preparing a bill. Aldrich knew what he wanted for his two cornerstones. And Warburg knew specifically what he wanted in the form of a central bank, for he had previously published his United Reserve Bank plan. The problem at Jekyll Island was to reconcile the conflicting conceptions of what ought to be done. There was no controversy as far as we know about the control problem. All agreed that the central bank should be controlled by the bankers and not by the government, though there was plenty of room between control by the banks and control by the government. The Jekyll Island meeting was a success. A tentative plan for banking reform emerged which became the basis for the Aldrich bill.

The remarkable feature of the Aldrich bill was how it came to be drafted. The National Monetary Commission was to study and report to Congress on needed banking reform. Autocrat that he was, Aldrich did not envision any substantive role for the commission members in drafting either the final report or the bill. Nor did he assign any significant role either to the House or Senate committees for banking legislation. The drafting of a bill was a matter for experts, not members of Congress inexperienced in banking and financial matters. The Aldrich strategy was to leave the work of preparing a report and a bill to himself and his chief aides, and then to keep members of the commission sufficiently informed about their progress to ward off any impending criticism. Only after the bill had been drafted did he show the bill to interested parties.

Unlike the case with other pieces of major legislation, the Congressional committees did not play an active role. There were no hearings to solicit

interested opinion prior to drafting the bill. The bill was put together, as
we have explained, by Aldrich himself and his New York banking associates at the clandestine Jekyll Island rendezvous. Aldrich was confident that
he could sidestep traditional procedures without jeopardizing the bill's
passage, but only if the Jekyll Island meeting remained absolutely secret.
The entire political hubbub about the fear of influence exercised by Wall
Street Aldrich ignored, inviting three of the most prominent New York
bankers to participate in the drafting of the bill. No more arrogant gesture
can be imagined. And only Senator Aldrich would have dared to pull it
off. He and his associates argued that every precaution had been taken in
the bill to keep the influence of Wall Street to a minimum and suggested
that the fear of Wall Street control was groundless! No one knew that Wall
Street bankers drafted the bill!

Despite Aldrich's efforts to the contrary, the bill was regarded as a partisan political measure identified not only with Senator Aldrich but the
Republican party as well. The Democratic platform specifically rejected
both the Aldrich bill and the idea of a central bank. And Carter Glass
never tired of insisting that the Democratic party had rejected the Aldrich
proposals.

HENRY DAVISON

Henry Davison (figure 2) had been a Morgan partner for less than two
years when, according to his biographer, he took the initiative to recommend to Senator Aldrich that a small group be assembled at the remote
Jekyll Island Club for the purpose of crystallizing ideas about banking
reform and perhaps formulating a draft of a bill. Lamont (1933, p. 97)
stated: "Senator Aldrich eagerly accepted Davison's suggestion and left
him to make up the party." It was Davison, not Aldrich, who selected the
participants.

Aldrich had invited Davison to be an adviser to the National Monetary
Commission; he accompanied commission members to Europe in the
summer of 1908 and aided in questioning European central bankers who
made themselves available for that purpose. He was not a technical adviser but "one who could bring to bear on the Commission's study a common sense knowledge of banking as it was practiced in the financial center of the United States."

What these skills were as specifically displayed at the Jekyll Island cabal
was later described by Warburg in Lamont (1933, pp. 98–99): "Warburg
emphasized Davison's uncanny personal skills in handling people and getting things done. Moreover, he was able to defuse awkward moments

Figure 2 Henry P. Davison

when tempers flared." As a "facilitator" he kept the discussion on track. We do not know what contributions he made to the technical discussion. His people skills were well known.

We have further evidence of his special skills in the role that he played during the 1907 panic. At the time he was vice president of the First National Bank, of which George Baker was the head. As the chief protégé of Baker he gained the attention of J. P. Morgan, who along with Baker and James Stillman took the initiative in proposing various panic preventive measures. In a long letter to Lamont (1933, p. 83) Benjamin Strong described Davison's contribution: "He was the commanding general over the forces in the field. Behind him was the general staff, primarily Mr. Morgan, Mr. Baker, and Mr. Stillman." And "It was in dealing with the human equation that Harry's supreme talent was shown. He reconciled different views, calmed the uneasy and anxious, he inspired the timid, sometimes disciplined the cowardly, but with it all his courage never flagged, his industry was unceasing and his good temper never failed him." These were the qualities especially admired by Morgan and later by

Aldrich, who observed Davison at his best while interviewing European
central bankers for the Monetary Commission and at Jekyll Island.

FRANK VANDERLIP

Frank Vanderlip (figure 3) was the chosen successor to James Stillman,
president of National City, the largest bank in New York. But at the time
of the Jekyll Island meeting he was still a vice president. Davison,
Vanderlip, and Warburg represented a younger generation of successful
bankers who were eager to assume the leadership mantle of their predecessors—Morgan, Stillman, and Baker. Davison and Warburg were partners
in two of the largest investment banking houses—Morgan's and Kuhn,
Loeb, and Co.

Vanderlip's preparation for his banking career was a sharp departure
from traditional practice. He was a journalist by profession, who had
served as a financial reporter for the *Chicago Tribune* and later became editor of the *Chicago Economist*. When Lyman Gage, a Chicago banker,
became secretary of the treasury, he invited Vanderlip to join him and later
serve as an assistant secretary. After his short stint at Treasury, James
Stillman offered him a position at National City Bank with a view to making him his successor. At the time of his appointment he had no experience as a commercial banker, but he was undeterred by his lack of knowledge. He (Vanderlip, 1935, p. 102) wrote in his memoirs: "I knew more
of the philosophy of banking than the whole bunch of them [officers of
the bank]. I had read and written and thought a great deal about our
banking system." At least two of the "eminent men" to whom he referred
were Adolph Miller, one of the first appointees to the Federal Reserve
Board, and J. Lawrence Laughlin. If there were no evidence to the contrary, guilt by association might place Vanderlip squarely in the real bills
camp, for Laughlin and Miller were both adherents of the real bills
doctrine.

His enthusiasm for banking reform was expressed as follows (1935, p.
181): "Ben Strong was equally zealous in his advocacy of change, and I
wrote articles, delivered speeches and argued with every banker with
whom I came in contact." He had played an active role in the Chamber
of Commerce committee to study currency and banking reform; he had
joined with them in the movement for banking reform by at least 1905,
if not earlier. As a member of the New York Committee in 1906 he had
joined in proposing a central bank as an alternative to Treasury control,
the use of the discount rate as the appropriate instrument for controlling
the expansion of bank credit, and an asset-based currency. He was also one

Figure 3 Frank A. Vanderlip

of the two Chamber of Commerce representatives to meet with the American Bankers Association considering banking reform. This latter committee recognized what was indeed remarkable at the time, that the issue of an asset currency did not entail a commitment to the strong form of the real bills doctrine. The committee considered the doctrine fallacious for the familiar reason that the same transactions could be the basis for a succession of commercial bills. We do not know whether Vanderlip agreed with the views of the committee, but if he did, it was a sharp turnabout from the views of his former teachers Miller and Laughlin.

PAUL WARBURG

Paul Warburg (figure 4), a member of a distinguished family of German bankers, moved to the United States in the fall of 1902 partly at the initiative of his American wife, Nina Loeb, daughter of the founder of Kuhn, Loeb and Co., investment bankers. He joined the investment banking firm as a general partner. His knowledge of European banking and of central banking in particular was unrivaled. From the time of the 1907 panic

Figure 4 Paul Warburg

Warburg began his campaign to reform the U.S. banking system. Shy at first and self-conscious about his German accent, he ventured slowly into the public arena. In speeches, articles in financial journals, and frequent contacts with leading New York bankers, he diagnosed our banking ills and suggested a remedy in the form of what he here called the United Reserve Bank, literally a blueprint of the technical clauses that were embodied in the Aldrich bill and later in the Federal Reserve Act. The United Reserve Bank was a central bank with 20 branches and a share capital of $100 million divided among the banks of the country, but dividends were limited to 4 percent. Local banking associations were to be created for the purpose of guaranteeing paper eligible for discount with the United Reserve Bank. The ideas of a central bank with branches financed by share capital with a fixed dividend were embodied in the Aldrich bill.

His most important recommendation, however, was the establishment of a discount market hitherto absent in the United States and, in his opinion, the cause of our banking woes. Most U.S. banks possessed no liquid asset upon which an elastic currency could be based. The promissory note—the credit instrument predominant among American bankers—was not a marketable asset and could not be disposed of easily in an emergency. The promissory note might be a "real bill," that is, a bill created for the specific purpose of financing goods in transit, presumably self-liquidating, but without endorsement. Warburg insisted that neither promissory notes nor any other bank asset could be liquidated in an emergency. The only ultimate source of liquidity in a banking or financial crisis was a central bank which was conspicuously absent in the United States before 1914. To establish a discount market, two revolutionary changes in American banking practice were necessary: (1) the replacement of the promissory note by a bill of exchange similar to bills of exchange in France, Germany, and Great Britain in the portfolios of commercial banks; and (2) the creation of a central bank that would stand ready to purchase these bills at the discretion of the seller. The two could not in his opinion be separated.

Warburg made it quite clear that profit should not be a prime motivating force in the operation of the United Reserve Bank. To avoid the possibility that earnings considerations would dictate behavior, he recommended that the government should contribute to the expenses of the United Reserve Bank such a lump sum that it will be able to pay shareholders the fixed 4 percent dividend.

In his 1930 book Warburg refers to the Jekyll Island meeting, though not by name. He wrote: "Though 18 years have gone by, I do not feel free to give a description of the most interesting conference concerning which Senator Aldrich pledged all the participants to secrecy." He knew that Stephenson's biography of Aldrich was about to be published. True to his word he does not tell us what went on at the conclave, but he did comment on Senator Aldrich as a person and as a politician. Warburg was especially impressed with Aldrich's nonpartisan approach. His great political power he attributed to "his indefatigable, painstaking willingness to ascertain the facts down to their last details." Although Aldrich seemed committed at the outset to a full-fledged central bank in the European sense, by the time the conference ended that rigid model had been abandoned. He indicated the items in the Aldrich bill with which he most disagreed— namely, the question of control. He preferred more government representation. He also took exception to a uniform discount rate.

Unlike the other Jekyll Island participants, at least some of Warburg's contributions are readily identifiable. Provisions of his United Reserve Bank proposal (March, 1910) appear directly in the Aldrich bill:

1. The creation of local associations and central bank branches
   in the cities where the head offices of the local associations
   were located

2. Share capital as a source of funding
3. Creation of a discount market with two-named commercial paper not having more than 28 days to maturity
4. Fixed dividends of 4 percent with excess earnings returned to the U.S. Treasury
5. Purchase and sale of government securities

The resemblance between the provisions of the United Reserve Bank and Aldrich's National Reserve Association was not a coincidence. There were quite a number of differences as well. Nevertheless, the main blueprint for the Aldrich proposals had been laid out by Warburg, and he deserves more credit than the rest for the so-called technical contributions.

A. PIATT ANDREW

A. Piatt Andrew (figure 5) was an assistant professor of economics at Harvard University when he was recruited by Aldrich at the recommendation of Harvard's President Charles W. Eliot to serve the National Monetary Commission in a variety of capacities: special assistant of the commission, consultant to Aldrich, research director and editor of more than 20 volumes sponsored by the commission. His more distinguished colleague at Harvard, Oliver Sprague, was also a money and banking specialist, but he had expressed earlier his opposition to a central bank. After completing his work for the commission Andrew did not return to Harvard. President Taft appointed him director of the mint in August 1909, and in the following year (June 1910) he became assistant secretary of the treasury. He was assistant secretary at the time of the Jekyll Island meeting.

In a special memorandum prepared for Stephenson's biography of Aldrich, Andrew indicated that on the journey commission members made to Europe to study European central banking practice, he attempted to acquaint them with the basic principles of money and banking. He wrote (Stephenson, 1930, p. 335): "Many of its members were no real students of monetary matters."

A parallel with Parker Willis, Carter Glass' assistant in the preparation of the Glass bill, readily suggests itself. Both were economists whose specialty was money and banking. Willis was the principal drafter of the Glass bill, whereas that responsibility fell collectively on the Jekyll Island participants. Willis was an adherent of the real bills doctrine. Andrew was not. Both acknowledged the origins of the proposed legislation in the Clearing House Associations in the United States.

Figure 5 A. Piatt Andrew

Andrew identified the multiple purposes of the Aldrich plan:

To prevent banking panics
To relieve seasonal stringencies in the money market
To control stock market speculation by the diversion of funds
from the money market
To make bank notes and reserves more responsive to business
needs
To provide new facilities for foreign trade

These objectives differed in no important ways from those of the Glass-Owen bill.

He predicted that the suggested banking reform would create a larger market for short-term obligations, a more restricted market for stock exchange collateral, lower rates for commercial paper and higher rates for call loans, greater stability of interest rates, and a gradual convergence of regional interest rates. He was perhaps overly sanguine when he said the country would never again be obliged to suspend cash payment, and the banks would always be able to convert their sound commercial paper into cash or immediately available funds and would do away with banking panics!

Andrew pointed out that the recognition of broader responsibilities of the clearinghouses to include banking stability was distinctly an American tradition without a European counterpart. Moreover, the issue of control was resolved by employing the device of the federal principle already embodied in our political structure. Andrew concluded (Stephenson, 1930, p. 28): "The proposed plan in its narrow outlines is only a perpetuation, legalization, and rationalization of the ingenious but illegal local makeshift in the past." The illegal makeshift to which he referred was the suspension of cash payment by the New York Clearing House.

These short sketches of the Jekyll Island participants are revealing. Senator Aldrich had recruited a younger generation of New York bankers as his special advisers but not without the implicit approval of Morgan, Baker, and Stillman. Vanderlip, Davison, and Warburg personified Wall Street; they represented two of the largest investment banking houses, Morgan's and Kuhn, Loeb and Co., and the largest commercial bank in the city. No one in the United States was better qualified than Warburg, whose knowledge of European banking and European central banks was unmatched. He had produced the first, detailed concrete proposal for a U.S. style central bank. And Vanderlip had gone on record as an advocate of a U.S. central bank. We have seen that Aldrich himself had become a convert to a central bank after the Monetary Commission's trip to Europe in the summer of 1908. The main issue, therefore, at Jekyll Island was not whether a central bank, but what kind. Aldrich had loaded the deck from the very outset. He also felt certain that the commission members would go along even if they had no idea how the Aldrich plan worked or by whom it had been devised. One of the great anomalies of U.S. financial history is how Wall Street bankers managed to play the role they did while politicians and the public were decrying Wall Street domination and influence! No one else but Aldrich would have attempted it. No one else would have succeeded.

Submission of Aldrich's suggested plan to the Monetary Commission in January 1911 was the occasion for the preparation of a strategy by Aldrich and his Jekyll Island associates to obtain broad political support. Included in the strategy was a campaign to educate the public on the necessity for banking reform. Warburg was instrumental in the formation of a National Citizens' League to serve such a purpose and to assure wide geographical participation. J. Lawrence Laughlin was enlisted to serve as executive director and to deflect attention away from Wall Street and the influence of the eastern financial interests. Laughlin, to the bewilderment of Warburg, conceived the league as nonpartisan and noncommittal about the Aldrich bill. Tension ran high between Aldrich's supporters over Laughlin's conception of why the Citizens' League had been created.

The strategy also included extensive speaking engagements by Senator Aldrich and his associates, especially to the large associations of bankers and businessmen. How successful the Aldrich strategy was in winning wide public support is still open to some dispute. But the campaign was highly successful in focusing public attention on banking reform and the leading issues in the debate. It contributed to molding public opinion favorably disposed to a U.S. style central bank, which would pay dividends when the Glass-Owen bill came up for consideration in 1913. When the Democratic administration assumed office in 1913, the groundwork had been laid by Aldrich and his supporters. All that remained to be done was to formulate a new proposal in the light of the preferences of the new administration.

THE ALDRICH PLAN

Barely two months after the Jekyll Island conclave Aldrich submitted a plan for banking reform to the National Monetary Commission entitled "Suggested Plan for Monetary Legislation." The pamphlet was dated January 16, 1911. It was not a bill in legislative format but an outline of the structure of a new financial institution called the Reserve Association of America, whose objectives could be achieved "without the creation of such a central bank" as existed in Europe. Aldrich modified his "Suggested Plan" in October 1911. The final report of the commission was sent to Congress in January 1912 along with a bill—the Aldrich bill—introduced in the Senate at the same time. Aldrich's original plan, the revised October version, and the formal 1912 bill were similar. A few important changes were made in each draft, but the substance remained unchanged. The name of the new institution was modified slightly from Reserve Association of America to National Reserve Association.

The January 1911 report muted the effect of the recommended changes by stating its aim was to liberalize the national banking system rather than to formulate a plan that would fundamentally change it. The Aldrich plan called for greater cooperation among the banks through a formalized structure, the effect of which should be the elimination of banking panics. The functions of the new institution included: to be the fiscal agent of the Treasury, the issue of paper money, the discount of commercial paper, centralization of the reserve, and the clearing and collection of checks.

The Aldrich plan for a central bank embodied two principles that distinguished the National Reserve Association from its European counterparts: the federal principle and democratic governance. Centralization and autocratic governance characterized European central banks. The division of the Aldrich system into local and district associations and a national association of banks reflected its federal structure, and the election of boards of directors by the member banks, its democratic control. A third principle—the principle of voluntarism—was reflected in the membership criteria. The earlier version of the Aldrich plan had confined participation to national banks on a purely voluntary basis with a minimum capital of $25,000. The October version extended membership to state bank and trust companies who were prepared to purchase stock in the association equal to 20 percent of their capital, the same as national banks. A fourth principle, if it may be called a principle, was embodied in the distribution of earnings, the principle of constrained profit maximization. Dividends were limited to 4 percent, additional earnings being apportioned to surplus with a fixed limit of 5 percent to shareholders; any excess beyond the specified distribution would accrue to the government in the form of a franchise tax.

Reflecting the federal principle, each participating bank belonged to a local association of banks no less than ten in number with a minimum capital of $5 million. The function of the local associations was to approve the application of each bank for a guarantee of the commercial paper that it desired to discount with the District Reserve Association. The local associations of banks were combined into 15 branches with the authority to discount notes and bills of exchange carrying the endorsement of the bank requesting the discount. These discounted notes would presumably have arisen out of commercial transactions having a maturity of no more than twenty-six days. The discount rate would be the same for all district branches. The authority, however, for raising and lowering the rates resides with the National Reserve Association, and not the separate branches. The function of the fifteen branches were: (1) to hold the reserves of the participating banks in the district; (2) to issue currency notes; (3) to discount paper; (4) to transfer balances between branches; and (5) to perform all operating functions including the clearing and collection of checks.

The principle of democratic control was embodied in provisions for the election of boards of directors at the local, district and national levels. At the base of the governance pyramid were local associations that elected a board of directors, three-fifths of whom were chosen on the one bank–one vote principle, the remaining two-fifths being chosen according to the number of bank shares, reflecting bank size. The selection of the directors of each of the fifteen branches was slightly more complex. Each local association would select one board member. In addition, a number of directors equal to two-thirds of the number of local associations within the district were selected, each bank having as many votes as its holding of shares in the National Reserve Association.

At the apex of the governance pyramid was the National Reserve Association, with power to set uniform discount rates, buy and sell securities, and supervise the operations of the fifteen branches. In the initial version there were forty-five directors of the National Reserve Association including six ex-officio members: the governor, two deputy governors, and the secretary of the treasury, secretary of commerce and labor, and the comptroller of the currency. An executive committee of nine members would be chosen by the directors and would be responsible for daily operations. The head of the association was the governor, who in the initial version would be chosen by the president from a short list submitted by the directors. In the original version he could be removed by the president. At the initiative of the ABA that was changed in the October version to removal by a two-thirds vote of the directors. None of the ex-officio cabinet members served on the Executive Committee.

The composition of the national board was modified in the final bill: fifteen directors were chosen by the branches to represent agriculture, commerce, industry and others; nine additional directors would be elected, with each branch casting as many votes as the number of shares held by the banks in that branch. A seventh ex-officio member was added, the secretary of agriculture. Control of the National Reserve Association was lodged with the banks. Although Aldrich acknowledged that the public had a vital interest in its behavior, control remained firmly in the hands of the bankers.

The Aldrich plan was an imaginative blueprint for a U.S. style central bank with distinguishing organizational and governance features. The fifteen branches were more than fifteen operating arms of the association. They were fully autonomous units in the administration of discounts, although they lacked the discretion to vary the discount rate. Banker control was manifest from the local to the national level. The whole governance apparatus was designed to minimize partisan political control as well as domination by a relatively small number of Wall Street banks. The Aldrich bill was the product of the clandestine Jekyll Island meeting of Wall Street bankers and not the work of members of the National Monetary Commission. The New York banks were able to exert more influence in molding a bank reform measure that anyone including themselves could have anticipated. Only Senator Aldrich could have carried off such a feat of political legerdemain.

CHAPTER SIX

THE GLASS BILL

The movement for banking reform suffered a temporary setback when the Aldrich bill was introduced in the U.S. Senate in January 1912 with no further action being taken. Although the momentum for banking reform had decelerated, some genuine progress had been made. Opposition to a central bank centered on what kind of central bank, not on whether to have one, and alternative asset-based currency proposals were shelved. No one could anticipate when banking reform would reappear on the legislative agenda. But it was clear that any congressional action would be delayed until after the presidential election in November. Two events put banking reform back on track, the selection of Carter Glass as chairman of the House Banking and Currency subcommittee to consider currency reform and then shortly thereafter his accession as chairman of the full committee, and the election of a Democratic president, Woodrow Wilson, who was sympathetic to banking reform. The leadership mantle had passed from Senator Aldrich to Representative Carter Glass, and we commence the third and final stage of the movement for banking reform.

WHO WAS CARTER GLASS?

Carter Glass (figure 6) was a Democratic congressman from Virginia who had served for ten years as a minority member of the House Banking and Currency Committee. Born in 1858, he had been elected to the House of Representatives in 1902 when he was forty-four years old. He emerged from obscurity when as a ranking Democrat he was directly in line to succeed Arsene Pujo of Louisiana as chairman of the committee.

Glass had no special qualifications for the challenging task awaiting him of formulating a banking reform bill. Not being a banker, he absorbed his

Figure 6 Carter Glass (photo courtesy of Robert Bachrach)

knowledge of banking and currency during his long years of service on the Banking and Currency Committee. He made up for this knowledge deficit by diligent study and the counsel of his legislative assistant H. Parker Willis, an economist who had taught at Washington and Lee University for eleven years while at the same time acting as a Washington correspondent for the *New York Journal of Commerce.*

As a man Glass was slight of stature—only 5 feet 4 inches tall, sandy-haired, having a frail physique and a speech peculiarity with the words flowing from the left corner of his mouth. Altogether he was not a very impressive figure. Nevertheless, he was endowed with driving energy, an astringent pen, and restless ambition. He was largely self-educated, having ended his formal schooling when he was only thirteen. Thereafter, he began on-the-job training, first as a printer's devil, then as a reporter, and later as editor and publisher of several daily newspapers in Virginia. He often referred to himself as a "mere country editor." His journalistic experience proved invaluable to him as a politician; he had mastered the art of responding incisively and effectively in his relationships with the public and with his House and Senate colleagues.

THE ORIGINS OF THE GLASS BILL

The Glass bill was a by-product of a congressional investigation into the concentration of financial power in Wall Street, the so-called Money Trust Investigation. The issue was separate and distinct from currency and banking reform as embodied in the Aldrich bill. The chairman of the House Rules Committee, Robert L. Henry of Texas, proposed a resolution (House Resolution 405) calling for an investigation of the management of the finances of many of the great industrial and railroad corporations that was being concentrated in the hands of a few large New York City banks. Specific activities were identified: the marketing of securities, interlocking directorates, and the operation of the New York Clearing House and the New York Stock Exchange. After consideration of the Henry resolution, the House Democratic caucus rejected it and substituted House Resolution 429 for the purpose of obtaining "full and complete information of the banking and currency conditions of the United States for the purpose of determining what legislation was needed." The issue in dispute was jurisdiction, that is, whether the investigation should be conducted by the House Rules Committee or the Banking and Currency Committee. Otherwise both resolutions were the same. House Resolution 504 amended 429 to extend the power of the committee.

To implement the House Resolution as amended, the chairman of the Banking and Currency Committee, Arsene Pujo, created two subcommittees in April 1912. James F. Byrnes (1912) of South Carolina, a member of the committee, confirmed the creation of the two subcommittees:

> The Banking and Currency Committee weeks ago was divided, 11 members of it being directed to make the Money Trust investigation and the other members being directed to consider the legislative features of the Aldrich-Vreeland banking scheme.

Pujo headed the subcommittee whose task was to conduct the Money Trust Investigation; the second was chaired by Carter Glass.

Willis (1923, p. 113) conjectured that the resolution creating the Money Trust Investigation "was the beginning of serious work on banking and currency by the Democratic party. . . ." Had Congress not made provision for the Money Trust Investigation, the work of Glass' subcommittee on banking and currency reform may not have been undertaken. Be that as it may, the Money Trust Investigation explains the timing and the occasion for the appointment of the Glass subcommittee on banking and currency reform. It may also have provided the wedge that led country bankers to withdraw their support for the Aldrich bill because of the revelations about the influence and control of a handful of New York financiers.

None of the House resolutions, neither 429 nor 504, contained any reference to currency reform. McCulley (1992, p. 263) stated that the Glass subcommittee "would draft any proposed banking legislation that the investigation indicated was necessary." But the Byrnes' statement went much further and included currency reform in the guise of a reconsideration of the Aldrich-Vreeland Act. There are, as far as I know, no records of the deliberations of the House Banking and Currency Committee with which to confirm or reject Byrnes' interpretation. If McCulley were correct, Glass and his subcommittee would have had to delay any action until the Money Trust Investigation proceeded far enough to have generated legislative remedies. But Glass and Willis began their work immediately to define the tasks of currency reform, that is, to provide a substitute for the Aldrich bill.

The first task according to Willis (1923, p. 132) was to compare the most recent bank reform proposals, namely the Muhleman, Fowler, and Aldrich bills. The subcommittee had agreed that the features embodied in these measures should serve as a basis for further consideration of the purely technical provisions of each of the three bills, provided that careful attention was paid to a noncentralized plan of organization that would ensure local control. Working out the full implications of local control would be the main task of Glass and the subcommittee. We discussed the Fowler and Aldrich bills in previous chapters. The Muhleman plan for a central bank did not appear until after Aldrich-Vreeland, but before the clandestine Jekyll Island conclave.

THE MUHLEMAN PLAN

In November 1909 Maurice Muhleman published the first of a series of articles in the *Banking Law Journal* (November, December 1909, January–March 1910) calling for the creation of a central bank. It received little or no attention at the time. Nevertheless, its historical significance lay in the fact that it was one of only three such proposals that Parker Willis (1923, p. 116) summarized for the consideration of the Glass subcommittee on the banking reform bill, and a number of its provisions appeared later in both the Aldrich and Glass-Owen bills. Unlike the Aldrich and Glass-Owen bills, Muhleman showed no reluctance to use the term "central bank"—even a politically charged Bank of United States that might draw an analogy with the unfortunate experience of the Second Bank of the United States.

Muhleman proposed a European style central bank with eighteen district branches and a capital stock of $100 million. Its purpose was to provide flexibility to the volume of currency, presumably during periods of seasonal strain and banking panics. The proposal was in a detailed legislative format including a discussion of the various provisions. Its characteristic features included one-quarter ownership by government in the Bank's capital stock, a feature not reproduced in either the Aldrich or the Glass-Owen bills, the remainder to be taken by the participating banks; the discount rate could not exceed 6 percent; the note issue could equal twice the amount of gold coin and bullion, any excess to be covered by commercial paper.

The "bill" did not discontinue the issue of national bank notes, but greenbacks were to be eliminated gradually. The note issue of national banks was limited to one-half of their capital stock. Muhleman conjectured that the volume of national bank note circulation would be reduced by $190 million and that $346 million of greenbacks would be retired from circulation.

The Muhleman plan contained provisions that appeared later in the Aldrich and Glass-Owen bills. Among those appearing in Glass-Owen were: discounted notes must have a maturity of 90 days; no interest paid on reserve deposits; staggered terms for directors of the central bank to guarantee independence from special and partisan interests; constraints on the payment of dividends; limits on direct loans to government; and a 40 percent gold reserve requirement against reserve deposits.

Among those appearing in the Aldrich bill were: provision for the establishment of branches, 18 in the Muhleman plan and 15 in the Aldrich bill; reserves of the participating banks could be held in part at the central bank and in part at reserve city and central reserve city banks; a board of directors of 45 in the Aldrich plan and 48 in the Muhleman bill; and voluntary membership for national and state banks and trust companies.

At the apex of the governance pyramid was a managerial board of 48 directors, 12 of whom were government directors appointed by the president with the consent of the Senate and 36 elected directors, 2 from each of the 18 districts. The directors were to elect a chairman, who would preside over meetings to be held at least once each quarter. The day-to-day operations would be in the hands of an executive committee of eight members, two of whom would represent the government. A governor and deputy governor would be appointed by the directors with the approval of the president for twelve-year terms. A manager of each branch would be appointed by the national board of directors.

The discount function was delegated to each branch. As we have stated, discounted paper was to have a maturity not to exceed ninety days and to have arisen out of commercial and industrial transactions. There is nothing in the discount provision that could be interpreted as real bills. Commercial paper available for rediscount "shall be duly endorsed by the banking institution tending the same shall have not more than 90 days to run to maturity and shall consist of either (a) bills of exchange or promissory notes bearing the name of at least one obliger in addition to the endorsement aforesaid, secured either by bills of lading for commodities in transit, or by receipts of duly supervised warehouses or elevators for commodities stored; or (b) bills of exchange or promissory note unsecured, bearing the name of more than one obliger in addition to the endorsement aforesaid; or (c) promissory notes bearing the names of at least one obliger in addition to the endorsement aforesaid, secured by collateral consisting of approved bonds, provided that advances upon such paper never be in excess of 80 percent. . . ."

The note issue function was the most detailed of the bill's provision. Following Bank of England practice, the Bank of United States would be separated into an issue and a banking department, with the latter having full responsibility for note creation. The amount of notes was supposed to equal the par value of any U.S. bonds in its possession and an additional amount not to exceed twice the amount of gold coin and bullion, any excess to be covered by commercial paper. The Bank could not purchase bonds to issue notes. There was no provision for open market operations.

What the three bills shared in common were constraints on the payment of dividends, serving as the fiscal agent of the Treasury, independence of the central bank from special and partisan interests, a large amount of autonomy for central bank branches or regional reserve banks, and an organization committee for the purpose of setting up the central bank.

During the spring of 1912, according to Willis (1923, pp. 133–34), after an informal discussion among members of the subcommittee, a tentative list of propositions had been agreed to:

1. Emergency currency plans embodied in the Aldrich-Vreeland Act should be abolished
2. What was needed was a permanent basis of banking organization
3. That organization should be modeled on the existing experience of the clearinghouse organizations
4. Framework provided by Aldrich-Vreeland should be given due consideration
5. Features of existing proposals should be incorporated when useful

6. New bill should seek to provide for cooperative action by accepting the principle of centralization and suitable governance oversight and control
7. Guaranty of bank deposits should be carefully considered

These general propositions were supposed to serve as guidelines to Willis in the preparation of a draft proposal during the summer and autumn of 1912. Further action depended upon the outcome of the impending November presidential election.

Since no record of these discussions was kept, we do not know why the emergency currency provisions of the Aldrich-Vreeland Act were rejected. But we can conjecture that it was the work of Glass, since he had been opposed to the Aldrich-Vreeland Act from its inception. The emergency currency provisions were an effective remedy for banking panics, as we have seen in a previous chapter (chapter 4). Willis did not clarify what was meant by the need for a more permanent basis for banking organization, one presumably that did not respond solely to banking panics. Asset-based currency proposals represented a permanent basis of bank organization by allowing banks to issue currency based on their general assets, a reversion to antebellum banking practice. The desire of the subcommittee to give careful consideration to the guaranty of bank deposits did not involve a change in organizational structure; it would have been implemented within the existing national banking framework. These general guidelines were not of much help in the construction of a banking reform bill. A whole host of questions remained unanswered: Who, for example, should subscribe to the share capital of a central bank, and how much? How centralized should the proposed central bank organization be? How many regional reserve banks were there to be, with what degree of autonomy? What was the role of profit maximization? All of these questions as well as many more remained to be answered.

Willis (1923, p. 143) stated that the first time the proposed bill was presented to the president-elect in December 1912 it provided "for the actual incorporation of local reserve banks which should represent the banks of the community in which they were situated." The number of such banks was not specified, perhaps as many as the number of reserve cities. He referred to these banks as "reserve banks" with power to discount, hold deposits, issue notes and engage in open market operations. The object of these reserve banks was to provide local control of the discount process—but that role did not differ from the one the branches played in the Aldrich bill. There was an elected board of directors for each branch, as well as each reserve bank.

The bill was presented to the president-elect for the second time in two months in February 1913; it provided for a Reserve Bank Organization Committee for the purpose of designating reserve districts. The number of Federal Reserve districts with a bank in each district should not be less than fifteen. Each national bank in each district was required to subscribe stock in a Federal Reserve bank equal to 20 percent of its paid-in capital. Membership for state-chartered banks was optional.

Glass scheduled hearings in January and February 1913 to consider banking reform while they were completing their work on the bill to be shown to President-elect Wilson. Willis (1923, p. 51) described the purpose of the hearings as that of: "ascertaining public opinion, and of comparing the draft which had already been made with the ideas of all those who were in position to express an influential opinion with regard to it." The hearings were not for the purpose of getting feedback on any bill before the Glass subcommittee. Members of the subcommittee were not privy to the work done by Willis and Glass. Since they had not seen the proposed bill, committee members had no focal point to address their questions to witnesses. Nor were the witnesses any better informed about the provisions of the bill being formulated by Glass and Willis.

It was obvious at various times during the hearings that Glass and Willis had directed their questions to specific provisions of the bill they were formulating. They repeatedly returned to the question of the advisability of creating divisional reserve banks. Nor did Glass tire of reminding witnesses that the Democratic platform opposed the Aldrich bill and a central bank, as a ploy for deflecting testimony favoring the Aldrich bill. And given that constraint, what banking reform measures would the witnesses recommend? Some members of the subcommittee were more interested in the merits of the guaranty of deposits than the creation of a central banking system.

The term of the Sixty-second Congress expired on March 4, 1913; the life of Glass' subcommittee expired as well. Nevertheless, Glass and Willis continued their work. Not only were new appointments to the House Banking and Currency Committee delayed for three months until June 1, but Glass' status remained up in the air until his appointment as chairman of the full committee was announced at the same time. While various drafts appeared between June and October, work by the subcommittee was put on hold during the congressional and presidential election, to be resumed if the outcome was favorable to the Democrats.

As early as May, Senator Robert Owen of Oklahoma, chairman of the Senate Banking and Currency Committee, had been invited to confer with President Wilson, Secretary of the Treasury McAdoo, and Chairman Glass. He was informed that a banking bill was being prepared. Willis briefed him on the contents of the bill that he and Glass had been working on.

President Wilson had under consideration three separate banking reform plans: (1) the Glass bill, (2) a bill prepared by McAdoo, and (3) Senator Owen's bill. He made his decision in favor of the Glass bill. After a series of conferences, Wilson disclosed the major features of the Glass bill on June 23, at which time he referred to the "Glass-Owen bill" (McCulley, 1992, p. 297). Why he chose the one it would be difficult to say, other than the joint sponsorship of the bill when it went to the Senate. It was not recognition of any major contributions by Senator Owen. After going through at least seven versions, the House of Representatives concluded their debate on the Glass bill on September 18. The bill passed the House by 287 aye votes and 85 nays, revealing the extent of the strong Republican support.

THE SENATE DEBATE

The debate shifted to the Senate. Willis (1923, p. 472) concluded that the "Senate debate while accomplishing little or nothing in actual results or changes in the language of the bill, was, as one of ten, often far superior to the general mental caliber of discussion of the lower chamber." Disagreement was largely confined to the number of Federal Reserve Banks. Some favored as few as four, others not more than twelve. There was still some support for allowing the public to subscribe to the capital stock of the Reserve Banks. And differences also arose over the selection of the directors of the Reserve Banks, that is, by government or by the participating banks. The substance of the House bill remained largely intact. The Senate Banking Committee reported the bill without a recommendation. The final vote was recorded with only a majority of 20 aye votes.

One of the more striking features of the Senate hearings and debates is how little attention was actually paid to the question: Was the proposed legislation a solution to the banking panic problem? For example, no one related the membership issue to the effectiveness of panic prevention. Did making membership voluntary for state banks and trust companies impair the Fed's response? How were the nonmember banks supposed to obtain accommodation in time of crisis? Among member banks, would the supply of commercial paper be adequate? Moreover, did the entire burden of panic prevention fall on the discount instrument? What role were open market operations supposed to play? There simply was no discussion or debate on the mechanics of panic prevention, and only an occasional reservation expressed about its effectiveness.

A conference committee was required to resolve the difference between the bills that passed the House and the Senate. The number of reserve banks could not exceed twelve; the subscription of stock of the individual member banks was reduced from 20 to 6 percent of capital and surplus; the dividend was increased from 5 to 6 percent; reserves against Reserve Bank deposits were increased from 33½ percent to 40 percent; charges for the collection of checks were left to the discretion of the individual Reserve Banks; the secretary of the treasury could at his discretion deposit funds in Reserve Banks; the comptroller of the currency was returned to the Federal Reserve Board, and Federal Reserve notes could not be used as reserves of member banks. The creation of a deposit insurance fund financed from surplus earnings was thrown out by the conference committee. The debate never focused on deposit insurance as a substitute panic prevention measure in lieu of a central bank. Considering how unpopular the measure was among bankers, it is remarkable that it survived that long.

MORAWETZ AND THE IDEA OF REGIONAL RESERVE BANKS

The idea of regional reserve banks was probably the most innovative feature of the Glass-Owen bill, but its significance can easily be exaggerated. The function of the regional reserve banks did not differ from central bank branches of the Muhlemann and Aldrich bills. They were alike inasmuch as they both bore full responsibility for the discount function; each branch or regional reserve bank had its own separate board of directors with considerable autonomy in carrying out its assigned tasks. Reserve Banks, however, had extended authority to change the discount rate and to engage in open market operations.

    Willis did not reveal the source of the provision in the Glass-Owen bill for autonomous, regional reserve banks. But we do know that Victor Morawetz (1909, 1911) set out a divisional reserve bank plan in 1909 which was more fully developed in 1911. He rejected the view that a single central bank was applicable to the United States. By reason of size alone and the diversity of business conditions, a central bank, he thought, was not feasible. In his opinion it would be more desirable to commence with the creation of divisional reserve banks that would form a central association for the purpose of regulating matters of common interest, mainly uniform rules and regulations for the conduct of business. The officers of the central association would be chosen by the divisional reserve banks, with each bank entitled to a number of votes proportionate to its capital. The power to control and regulate the note issue would be vested in the national association.

    Willis and Glass had invited Morawetz to testify before the Glass subcommittee in January 1913, at which time Willis learned of the Morawetz divisional reserve proposal, if he was not already acquainted with it. Morawetz (1911, p. 153) maintained that objections to a single central bank for the United States did not apply to the creation of banks in different sections of the country that were "to act as national depositories for bank reserves and, in a measure, to perform the functions of sectional central banks." If it were found advisable sometime in the future to establish a single central bank, he thought the divisional banks could be made into branches. Each divisional bank would have its own share capital contributed by the participating national banks. Each national bank could keep its reserves either in its own vault or in the reserve banks. He also thought it desirable to pay interest on reserve deposits and to fix a maximum rate allowable on such deposits. Short-term commercial paper would be the sole earning asset of the divisional reserve banks, apparently precluding open market operations.

Willis (1923, p. 278) prepared a report for Chairman Glass and the subcommittee in which he echoed the same conclusions as Morawetz, that is, a single central bank was not necessary and may not be desirable. He stated "It is therefore necessary to abandon the idea of a single central banking mechanism for the United States." In its place there would be regional reserve banks individually organized and individually controlled, with their own capital and governance board, and with authority to make discounts and advances and to engage in open market operations.

THE CLEARINGHOUSE IDEA

The clearinghouse in the United States evolved as a voluntary association of banks in large commercial centers for the explicit purpose of the clearing and collection of checks. It was an institution designed to foster cooperation and collective action among the participating banks in an atmosphere dominated by individual self-interest. Glass (1927, p. 240) attributed the origin of the Federal Reserve System to the generic idea drawn from the organization of clearinghouses. The Aldrich bill report (1911) did likewise: "It is in effect an evolution of the clearing-house idea extended to include an effective central organization." Both Glass and Aldrich acknowledged the role that the idea of the clearinghouse played in planting the seed that shaped banking reform.

What was so compelling about the clearinghouse idea, however, was not spelled out clearly. Although the clearinghouse provided the basis for bank cooperation, there was no explicit coordination among the various clearinghouses. The leading clearinghouses in Boston, New York,

Philadelphia, and Chicago had devised a strategy to cope with banking panics. They authorized the issue of clearinghouse loan certificates. Banks that accumulated a deficit at the clearinghouse could discharge that debt by the issue of loan certificates, thereby conserving the stock of specie and legal tender currency and making possible the expansion of loans. Substantial quantities of clearinghouse loan certificates were issued during the banking panics in 1873, 1893, and 1907. The issue of certificates did not, however, prevent a suspension of cash payment. Although the issue of certificates conserved the cash reserves of the clearinghouse banks, it did not prevent interior banks from withdrawing their balances from clearinghouse banks, thereby precipitating the suspension of cash payment. Though not a fail-safe device for preventing banking panics, it did serve a useful function of panic moderation. Cooperation only went so far. In 1860, 1861 and 1873, the New York Clearing House allowed the banks to pool their reserves. Surplus reserves were redistributed to banks with a deficit. Reserve equalization worked successfully in 1860 and 1861 to ward off the suspension of cash payment, but failed to do so in 1873. I have described the reserve pooling arrangement more fully elsewhere (Wicker, 2000). There is no evidence that either Glass or Aldrich had any knowledge of the reserve equalization scheme. But they were well aware of the role played by clearinghouse certificates during banking panics. What impressed them the most was the role of collective action.

The clearinghouse, especially the New York Clearing House, had early on grasped the significance of the New York banks as holders of the country's ultimate banking reserve. After 1873 all efforts at reserve pooling were abandoned and faded from the collective memory. The clearinghouse had demonstrated that collective action was feasible and pointed in the direction that banking reform could be expected to go. The function of clearinghouses should be broadened, it was thought, and the number expanded to fit the needs not only of banks in commercial centers but elsewhere as well.

The "generic idea" Glass had in mind presumably included at the base a number of local associations of banks performing specific mechanical functions within bounded geographical areas and in response to local needs. These associations acquired panic prevention responsibilities. Moreover, they devised a financial instrument, the loan certificate, which enabled banks with deficits to borrow from the surplus banks, a forerunner of the discount mechanism embodied in the Aldrich and Glass-Owen bills.

Some advocates of banking reform proposed a simple extension of the function of the clearinghouses to the issue of currency notes on the basis of the general assets of the participating banks. The appeal of the idea lay in not requiring major restructuring of the national banking system. As early as 1903, Senator Orville Pratt had proposed such a plan. The idea resurfaced in 1906 in the report of the New York Chamber of Commerce. The emphasis accorded the clearinghouse idea was a deliberate effort to discover the underpinnings of banking reform in American banking practice, rather than simply adopting a European import, that is, a European style central bank.

Glass's generic idea has been pursued further by recent consideration of the origins of the Federal Reserve System. Gary Gorton (1985, p. 277) has claimed: "It is almost literally true that the Federal Reserve system, as originally conceived, was simply the nationalization of the private clearinghouse system." He maintained that clearinghouses looked much like central banks and arose endogenously in response to common problems faced by the banking industry.

As we have shown, the Aldrich bill owed little or nothing to the clearinghouse idea. The Jekyll Island cabal drew its inspiration from European style central banks modified to fit an American context. To associate, as Glass probably did, the clearinghouse system with regional reserve banks was a leap in the dark. The contribution of Victor Morawetz, even if unacknowledged by Glass and Willis, was probably far more important, and the clearinghouse idea an afterthought. Timberlake (1984, p. 14) concluded that the clearinghouse system proved so effective that he was led to wonder why the system had been rejected. That could equally have been said of reserve pooling!

Toma (1997, p. 26) attempted to attribute fundamental changes in monetary institutions to public finance considerations. The government's revenue requirement might create a demand for seigniorage. If the demand for seigniorage increased, the case could be made for a central bank; if the demand was weak, a competitive clearinghouse system might have been more appropriate. During the Great Debate on banking reform, the demand for seigniorage was correspondingly weak, thereby leading to the creation of what Gorton referred to as a Federal Reserve System that was simply a nationalization of the clearinghouse system. Timberlake (1993, p. 249–50) agreed. There was no need for discretionary policy by a government agency: "the early Federal Reserve System, operating on a real-bills principle . . . was to be a self-regulating appendage to a more fundamental self-regulating system—the operational gold standard." The Federal Reserve System, according to Timberlake, was originally intended to be a self-regulating clearinghouse system operating on a real bills basis. That is all very well if the major premise is true, that the Fed was supposed to operate on the real bills principle. But as we intend to show, both the Aldrich and Glass-Owen bills were real bills neutral. However, before we proceed to reexamine the theoretical underpinnings of the Aldrich and the Glass-Owen bills, we need to make a detailed comparison of the main provision of both bills. Their similarities are too striking to be attributable to mere coincidence, and should reveal the extent of the indebtedness of Glass-Owen to its precursor, the Aldrich bill.

CHAPTER SEVEN

THE ALDRICH AND GLASS-OWEN BILLS COMPARED

The failure of the Aldrich bill to make any further progress in Congress did not presage the end of the banking reform movement. Momentum was quickly rekindled with the election of Woodrow Wilson, who was an ardent advocate of banking reform. The baton passed from Nelson Aldrich to Carter Glass. Although the Democratic platform had rejected the Aldrich bill, the foundations had been laid for a U.S. style central bank, albeit one with some—though not all—objectionable features. Glass and his associate Willis could begin immediately with the task of drafting an alternative measure acceptable to the new Democratic administration, a task needless to say made easier by the work of their predecessors. With the Aldrich bill as a guide, they could incorporate the noncontroversial provisions and revise those that were objectionable, namely those dealing with governance. What emerged, as we shall shortly see, were striking resemblances between the provisions of the two bills. The similarities extended to how capital was to be raised, dividend constraints, discount operations lodged in regional and branch banks, discounts based on legitimate commercial and industrial transactions of short duration, an asset-based note issue, and federal and democratic organizational features. Warburg's (1930, Vol. 1, Chapter 8) line-for-line comparison of the provisions of the two bills revealed not only the similarities of substance but wording as well! We begin by comparing earnings provisions.

EARNINGS

One of the first problems to be resolved was the source of funds for establishing a central bank, that is, the amount of capital required. There were at least three separate and distinct sources for raising capital: (1) funding by the participating banks, (2) funding by government, and (3) funding by the public or some combination of the three. Capital could be raised by the purchase of shares by government and the public. Both were rejected in favor of funding by the participating banks in the Aldrich and Glass-Owen bills; banks would be required to purchase shares as a proportion of their capital stock. The Aldrich bill specified a fixed amount of share capital amounting to $200 million, whereas Glass-Owen only provided for a minimum capital requirement of $4 million for each Federal Reserve Bank.

Share purchases created expectations of dividends and participation in governance as a prerogative of "ownership." However, the prerogative of ownership was sharply curtailed; it did not extend to full participation in governance. The corporate governance analogy cannot be carried too far. Capital tied up in the central bank had an opportunity cost. The payment of dividends would compensate partially for the loss in earnings; it would also act as an incentive to participate.

The role of profit considerations in the operation of the National Reserve Association and the Federal Reserve System remained ambiguous. Profit maximization was not ruled out by legislative provision except to the extent that the payment of dividends was constrained to a fixed maximum percentage. Earnings not allocated to dividends would accrue to government in the form of a franchise tax. Neither bill provided any clear guidance about the role of earnings of the central bank. It was more or less a clearly understood interpretation of both bills that the central bank was supposed to meet current expenses out of current earnings. Shortfalls could be temporarily sustained from a contingency fund in the Aldrich bill and a surplus provision in Glass-Owen. The Aldrich bill contingency fund was not to exceed $2 million and was to act as a cushion to prevent current losses, if any, from impacting monetary policy considerations. In the 1920s some Federal Reserve Banks had insufficient earnings to pay dividends; some of them resorted to open market operations to make up the deficiency, which was not always consistent with broad policy objectives. In neither the Congressional debates nor hearings on the Glass-Owen bill was there a perception of a possible conflict between earnings and policy-related considerations. Warburg (1930, Vol. 1, p. 409) maintained that had the Federal Reserve Act allowed reasonable interest charges on checks in the process of collection, the need for Federal Reserve Banks to purchase government securities for earnings purposes would have vanished. The whole problem disappeared with the growth of earnings and never again led to potential policy conflicts.

DISCOUNTS AND OPEN MARKET OPERATIONS

Though never made explicit, one of the purposes of both the Aldrich and the Glass-Owen bills was to create a national discount market, identifying in general terms financial instruments through which the market could be accessed, thereby providing the banks with a much welcomed source of liquidity. Participating banks could request accommodation based on legitimate transactions of short maturity drawn from agricultural, industrial, or commercial purposes, terms of 28 days in the Aldrich bill and 90 days in Glass-Owen. The discount provision of the Aldrich bill was less rigid than the similar provision of the Federal Reserve Act. With the approval of the secretary of the treasury and the endorsement of the bank's local association, any direct obligation of the borrowing bank was eligible for discount, a provision that might be particularly helpful during banking panics.

The fifteen branches and the eight–twelve regional Reserve Banks were granted autonomy in the administration of the discount window. The authority to lend to member banks was vested in each of the branches and regional Reserve Banks. Application for accommodation had to be approved by a local association of banks of which it was a member under the terms of the Aldrich bill. Regional Reserve Banks had the authority and the discretion to lend to the member banks in its district. The power to change the discount rate differed between the two bills. Under the Aldrich bill the National Reserve Association set the discount rate without branch participation, whereas in the Glass-Owen bill the power resided with each Reserve Bank, with the approval of the Federal Reserve Board in Washington.

Similarly, the Aldrich bill empowered the National Reserve Association to engage in open market operations, but the Glass-Owen bill reposed that power in the individual Federal Reserve Banks. The 1913 Federal Reserve Act made no provision for coordinating the purchase and sale of securities by the individual Reserve Banks. An informal committee without legal status was organized by Governor Benjamin Strong of the Federal Reserve Bank of New York in 1923.

The technical provisions with respect to discounting and open market operations were almost identical in substance and wording. Where the two bills differed was in the authority to change the discount rate and engage in open market operations. The Reserve Banks had a greater degree of authority than the individual branches of the National Reserve Association, but the differences were matters of degree.

RESERVES

One of the alleged weaknesses of the national banking system was the pyramiding of reserves. Interbank deposits were allowed to satisfy part of the reserve requirement. For example, country banks (a reserve classification) were required to hold 15 percent of their deposits as reserves, three-fifths of which could be deposited with reserve city and central reserve city banks, the remainder being held in the banks' own vaults. Reserve city banks had to hold a 25 percent reserve, one-half of which could be deposited in central reserve city (New York, Chicago, St. Louis) banks. Central reserve city banks held a 25 percent reserve. The effect of the pyramiding of reserves was to transmit currency shocks immediately from country and reserve city banks to New York. Reserves, as a matter of fact, were not decentralized; they were highly concentrated in an exceedingly small number of New York banks holding the bulk of bankers' balances. The problem as Laughlin conceived it was the inelasticity of the stock of reserves. The remedy lay in a more flexible reserve supply mechanism through discounting and open market operations, a characteristic feature of both the Aldrich and Glass-Owen bills. Neither bill provided for discretionary changes in the reserve ratio as a policy instrument. But such changes were not ruled out in the Aldrich bill; unlike the Glass-Owen bill, there was no provision for a mandated reserve requirement ratio; the Executive Committee of the National Reserve Association had the power to fix its size.

Like the National Banking Act, the Aldrich bill permitted interbank balances to be counted as part of the reserve requirement, thereby inhibiting the concentration of bank reserves in branches of the National Reserve Association. On the other hand, the Federal Reserve Act, after calling for a 36-month transition period, concentrated reserves in the eight–twelve Reserve Banks, although vault cash could be counted as well. One of the purposes of the Federal Reserve Act was to concentrate the nation's gold reserve in a central reservoir, thereby relieving the Treasury of that responsibility.

NOTE ISSUES

The debate over an asset- versus a bond-secured currency had been resolved in the Aldrich-Vreeland Act in 1908. Participating banks were authorized to issue currency notes on the basis of commercial paper in periods of emergency. This aspect of an asset-based currency was embodied in both the Aldrich and Glass-Owen bills. The note issue privilege, however, resided in the National Reserve Association in the Aldrich bill and in the Federal Reserve Board acting through a Federal Reserve agent in each Federal Reserve Bank in the Glass-Owen bill. The details of the note issue were left vague, presumably through the fifteen branches of the Aldrich bill. Commercial paper, bills of exchange, and gold were the basis for the note issue in the Aldrich bill. If the reserve fell below 50 percent, the National Reserve Association would be subject to a special graduated tax. In the event the ratio fell below 33½ percent, no additional notes could be issued. The total note issue was capped at $900 million. Any issue above that amount was subject to a graduated tax. All notes were fully exchangeable into gold. Federal Reserve notes were also backed by 100 percent in commercial paper and an additional 40 percent gold reserve. The Glass-Owen bill contained no cap on the amount of notes issued except the commercial paper/gold reserve constraint. Nor was there a provision that Federal Reserve notes were convertible freely into gold.

It was certainly clear that a central bank had never been demonstrated to be a superior mechanism for the issue of bank notes compared to an asset-based currency. With an asset-based currency the initiative to increase the bank note circulation rested solely with the national bank suffering the currency drain; its response was predictable. The bank may have had no other option. The response of a central bank was less predictable, especially if it was not properly organized and managed, resulting in delays in recognition and undertaking action. Nor would the issue of notes be any safer. *Bankers Magazine* (1907, p. 315) concluded on the basis of the available evidence that an asset-based currency issued by national banks would be perfectly safe, and the establishment of a central bank could scarcely be defended as any safer. If removing bank note inelasticity was the sole purpose of banking reform, then an asset-based currency might be preferable. The debate about an asset-based currency did not focus on whether or not the note issue was a responsibility of the government or private banks. It did play an important role in the decision about what functions to grant a U.S. style central bank.

One other difference remained, but it was without practical significance. National Reserve Association notes were obligations of the National Reserve Association, whereas Federal Reserve notes were obligations of the U.S. government at William Jennings Bryan's insistence. Wilson and Glass agreed to go along with this residue of the old populist currency wars of an earlier time. Safety of the note issue remained a preoccupation of the formulators of both bills. Equal consideration was not given to the safety of checking account deposits.

ORGANIZATIONAL STRUCTURE

Both the Aldrich and the Glass-Owen bills provided for a decentralized operating structure. The Aldrich bill divided the country into fifteen districts with a branch in each district. The Glass-Owen bill created no less than eight nor more than twelve districts with a Reserve Bank in each district. Each district branch of the National Reserve Association and each Reserve Bank had its own board of directors, which as we have seen had the authority to administer the discount mechanism. Reserve Banks had the additional authority to set the discount rate and to engage in open market operations. The principal operating functions of a central bank were performed by the branches and the Reserve Banks. The idea of a regional system of quasi-autonomous reserve banks did not originate with the Federal Reserve Act. Embodied in the Aldrich bill was a system of fifteen separate districts with a branch bank in each district. The word "branch" was unfortunate, for it did not have the same connotation as when applied to the Bank of France, the Bank of England, and the Reichsbank. There were 11 branches of the Bank of England, 188 branches of the Bank of France, and 93 so-called head branches of the Reichsbank. At the Bank of France and the Bank of England the local branch management had full control of discounts, not including the rate of discount. Assisting the manager of a Bank of France branch was a local board of directors from "the best qualified commercial, industrial, and agricultural representatives in the region." Managers of the branches of the Bank of France were named by the chief of state on the report of the minister of finance upon presentations made to him of three candidates by the governor of the Bank. Managers of the Bank of England were named by the Court of Directors of the Bank.

Not only did the two bills differ about the degree of autonomy of the district banks, there were differences concerning compulsory or voluntary membership of the participating banks. Membership was purely voluntary for national and state banks and trust companies in the Aldrich bill and compulsory only for national banks in Glass-Owen. Another minor difference arose over the designated fiscal agent of the Treasury. Under the Aldrich bill the National Reserve Association was the mandated fiscal agent of the Treasury. Glass-Owen made it obligatory for the Reserve Banks to act as fiscal agents when required by the Secretary of the Treasury, but he retained the discretion to deposit funds outside the Reserve System.

The National Reserve Association and the Federal Reserve Board were entrusted with purely supervisory functions. But these powers were specifically constrained in the Glass-Owen bill. There were no similar constraints in the Aldrich bill. Both bills were silent on the broad objectives of monetary policy, but preservation of the gold standard was implicit.

GOVERNANCE STRUCTURE

The similarity of wording and substance between the two bills is striking, but we do not wish to obscure the differences. Nowhere are those differences more glaring than in the provisions defining governance of the central bank. The one question that attracted the greatest controversy was: Who was going to control the central banking system, the bankers or government appointed officials? The Aldrich bill provided for a scheme of governance at every level where banker control was dominant. Participating banks were, first, members of a local association. In the final version of the bill, these local associations were organized into fifteen districts with a branch in each district having a board of directors elected from the affiliated banks. The fifteen branches were united into a National Reserve Association with a board of forty-six directors: fifteen from the branches (one from each branch); an additional fifteen who were supposed to represent agriculture, commercial, industrial, and other interests; nine chosen by the branches on the principle that the number of votes was to equal the number of shares; and ex-officio members including the governor of the National Reserve Association, two deputy governors, the secretaries of the treasury, agriculture, commerce, and labor, and the comptroller of the currency. The governor was to be selected by the president of the United States from a list submitted by the board of directors. An executive committee, or policy committee, was composed of nine members, the governor, two deputy governors, the comptroller of the currency, and five directors representing the participating banks. By omitting cabinet members, their influence was muted.

The Glass-Owen bill in its final version sharply curtailed the representation of banker interests at both the district and national levels. Each district reserve bank had a nine-member board of directors, only three of whom were bankers; three were required to be engaged in commerce, agriculture, or some other industrial pursuit. The remaining three were "public" members appointed by the Federal Reserve Board in Washington. Nevertheless, there was banker representation, albeit not controlling, at the district level. But banker representation was completely eliminated at the national level. The central controlling agency, the Federal Reserve Board, included two ex-officio members, the secretary of the treasury and the comptroller of the currency, and five members appointed by the president with the consent of the Senate.

Central banks are by their very nature political institutions that impact the well-being of the public for good or ill. When central banks act to curb inflation, reduce unemployment, and promote economic growth, some are harmed; there are political consequences that cannot be ignored; policymakers must assess the political consequences of their actions; central banks must be accountable to the public. Nor can the process ever be free of "politics" in the above sense.

What supporters of the Aldrich bill feared was the injection of political considerations into central bank decision making. What they intended, to be free of "politics," meant to be free from political party influence. These same supporters could not conceive of presidential appointees not governed by partisan politics. Supporters of the Glass-Owen bill equally could not fathom how banker control and banker self-interest would always coincide with the wider public interest. The rejection of the Aldrich bill and its replacement by the Glass-Owen may be viewed, not incorrectly, as a political accident, the accident, that is, of the Wilson presidency and his undaunted insistence on government control of the central banking system.

These differences about governance of the central bank were not simply ideological. Granted there were deeply entrenched views about the role of government in economic affairs. Supporters of the Aldrich bill associated government intervention with the threat that purely partisan political considerations would be decisive. For example, giving the president the authority to appoint Federal Reserve Board members was an invitation to inject "politics" into central bank management. "Politics" meant partisan bias, which was unacceptable. And the only way to keep the central bank free of politics in the partisan sense was to legislate banker control.

There were provisions of the Aldrich bill that recognized the public interest aspects of central banks. The president appointed the governor, but only from a preferred list submitted by the forty-five directors of the National Reserve Association. Moreover, secretaries of the treasury, agriculture, commerce and labor and the comptroller of the currency were made ex-officio members of the board of directors, but did not serve on the nine-man executive committee. Representation of public officials was token at best. As we know, President Wilson was not inclined to support a bill in the absence of government control. His position was even stronger than that of Carter Glass, who had no problem with accepting banker representation on the Federal Reserve Board. In fact banker representation was included in an earlier version of the Glass bill. To a group of bankers Wilson allegedly quipped: "Who would place a representative of the railroads on the Interstate Commerce Commission?"

Central banks, to repeat, by their very nature cannot be free of politics in the sense their actions impact the well-being of the public. There are benefits and costs distributed unequally when the central bank acts to restrain inflation, curb stock market speculation, or foster economic growth. Some people benefit, others are harmed, from which political consequences ensue. The central bank is a political institution which can act with various degrees of autonomy from the conventional political arena. The question is the extent and degree of central bank accountability to the public.

The process of selecting sites for the location of Reserve Association branches and Federal Reserve Banks was the same. Both bills provided for the appointment of an Organization Committee whose task it was to determine district locations. The membership of the two committees was almost identical: the secretary of the treasury and agriculture together with the comptroller of the currency were members of both committees. The secretary of commerce and labor was included in the Aldrich bill but omitted in the Glass-Owen bill. The two bills shared the same criterion for the selection of districts. They would be drawn with "due regard to the convenience and customary course of business and not necessarily along state lines."

THE ALDRICH-GLASS LEGACY

A series of necessary steps had to be taken before a central bank could be established in the United States. The historical prejudice against a central bank dating from the antebellum period and the Jackson-Biddle feud had to be dispelled and a nationwide educational campaign conducted to demonstrate the feasibility of a U.S. style central bank. Moreover, the protagonists of an asset-based currency issued by national banks had to be convinced of the superiority of a central bank. What this meant in fact was the abandonment of the principle of an asset-based currency that had dominated all of the measures for banking reform between 1894 and 1908.

By 1910 Aldrich and his associates could claim a modicum of success. The central bank shibboleth no longer was an obstacle to the creation of a central bank. Proponents of an asset-based currency had been silenced, and public opinion tilted in favor of a central bank. But the Aldrich bill when introduced in the Senate in 1912 was stillborn, a casualty of Democratic opposition and divisiveness within the Republican ranks. Aldrich's efforts, however, had not been in vain. Carter Glass and his associate H. Parker Willis, as we have shown, relied heavily on the Aldrich bill in drafting the Federal Reserve Act.

The argument we have been making is that Senator Aldrich deserves equal billing with Carter Glass as a founder of the Federal Reserve System once we remove the ambiguity about the term "founder." Founder of the Federal Reserve in a strictly narrow sense may refer to the person or persons directly responsible for the Federal Reserve Act and who steered it successfully through Congress. There is no ambiguity about who that person was—Carter Glass, chairman of the House Banking and Currency Committee. In a broader sense, though, founder may also refer to the person or persons responsible for making a central bank the focus of banking reform and drafting a bill that served as the basis both in substance and wording for the Federal Reserve Act. The groundwork was laid by Senator Aldrich and his associates between 1908 and 1912.

The debt of the Glass-Owen bill to its precursor the Aldrich bill was not only not acknowledged but also repudiated by Glass and Willis because of an unfortunate set of circumstances. Glass and Willis exaggerated their claims that the Glass-Owen bill owed nothing to the Aldrich bill. Aldrich himself was not entirely blameless; he launched a scathing denunciation of the Glass-Owen bill. Emotions were running high, and a sober assessment could not be expected from either of the interested parties. Glass (1927, p. 239) concluded: "the Federal Reserve has no relationship to the Aldrich plan beyond a common use in some cases of indispensable banking technique and nomenclature." And Willis' (1923, pp. 523–24) repudiation was even stronger: "1) The Federal Reserve Act was not a copy or derivative of any other bill; 2) It had little relationship in principle to the so-called Aldrich bill, although in various places made use of the language of the Aldrich bill on matters relating to technique; and 3) It was not derived from, or modified after or influenced even in the most remote way by other bills or proposals currently put forward from private sources but, on the contrary, it was itself the pattern from which a host of imitators sought to copy." Glass and Willis' reluctance to acknowledge any influence of the Aldrich bill may have stemmed from a plank in the Democratic party platform which specifically opposed "the Aldrich bill or a central bank." It may also explain why Glass denied that the Federal Reserve constituted a central bank. Glass' approach to the Aldrich bill, however, went much deeper. Like Wilson he favored government control rather than banker control of the central bank, but unlike Wilson he did not oppose banker representation on the supervisory board.

One may ask, does it really matter whether there were one or two founders of the Fed? Absent the role of Senator Aldrich we get an exaggerated picture of the Glass achievement. He did little to bring business, banker, and public opinion around to focus on the desirability of a central bank instead of an asset-based currency. The Glass contribution was essentially legislative. He did what no other politician had been able to do, namely steer legislation successfully through the House and the Senate. But it was Aldrich, not Glass, who paved the way for the transition to a U.S. style central bank.

Moreover, absent the role of Aldrich, we seriously underestimate the contribution that the New York bankers, especially Paul Warburg, played in the design of a U.S. central bank. It was the Jekyll Island cabal that applied the principles of federalism and democracy to the problem of organization and governance of the central bank, principles later incorporated into the Glass-Owen bill. The New York bankers got all they wanted, with the single exception of banker control.

There is a striking parallelism between the wording and substance of the discount provision of both the Aldrich and Glass-Owen bills. Yet each has been subject to conflicting interpretations. According to West (1977, p. 158) the real bills doctrine was the cornerstone of the Federal Reserve Act. We will have more to say about this in the next chapter, which continues our comparison of the provisions of both bills.

CHAPTER EIGHT

THEORETICAL
UNDERPINNINGS

The canonical interpretation of the origins of the Fed is that its theoretical underpinnings resided in the real bills doctrine. This attribution is usually credited to Parker Willis and Lloyd Mints. Willis as chief consultant to Carter Glass and the House Banking and Currency Committee was largely responsible for drafting the Glass-Owen bill. Not only was he a professed adherent of the real bills doctrine, he attested repeatedly to its importance in shaping the Federal Reserve Act. Mints (1945, p. 9) concluded that real bills "was the main reliance of the agitation for banking reform in the United States before 1913." A restatement of that hypothesis appeared more recently in the works of West (1977) and Timberlake (1984). With the benefit of accumulated research and insight on the origins of the Aldrich bill and its surprisingly close relationship to the Glass-Owen bill, we can see now that the extent of that influence was probably exaggerated. The Federal Reserve Act itself, as we propose to show, was in the strong sense real bills neutral.

REAL BILLS AND THE FED'S ORIGIN

The real bills doctrine is a theory of bank liquidity that states bankers should make only short-term self-liquidating loans created for the specific purpose of providing funds for producing, purchasing, carrying, or marketing of goods. Self-liquidating loans were supposedly loans made, for example, for financing the short-term working capital needs of business where the proceeds of the sale of the final product would ensure repayment. The amount of credit would presumably adjust automatically to quantity demanded without any harmful effects of inflation; no regulation or interference by government is warranted. There is both a strong and weak form of the doctrine. The strong form stresses automaticity; attention to quality alone is sufficient. The weak form does not require automaticity. Quality remains paramount and loans for purely speculative and long-term investment purposes are excluded. The doctrine in its strong form is fallacious. When bankers continue to make loans for whatever purpose, inflation will be the result after full resource utilization is reached.

The roots of the theory can be traced to early nineteenth-century Britain. Two opposing schools of thought differed about how or whether to control the note issue. The Banking School maintained that the note issue ought to expand and contract in response to the needs of business, which would be the case if banks confined their activities to short-term commercial and industrial purposes. The currency would adjust automatically to the ebb and flow of trade. On the other side were writers of the Currency School, who rejected the Banking School view as fallacious. They thought the note issue should vary precisely as a pure specie circulation and that the exchanges were the appropriate guide to regulating the note issue.

The evidence for what influence the real bills doctrine exerted can presumably be found in: (a) the language of the Federal Reserve Act itself, (b) the views of the framers of the act, and (c) Fed policymakers' behavior in the formative years. We will examine each in turn. The discount provision is the relevant provision of the Federal Reserve Act in which to discern real bills influence. Section 13 authorized the Federal Reserve Banks to: "discount notes, drafts and bills of exchange arising out of actual transactions, that is, notes, drafts, and bills of exchange issued or drawn for agricultural, industrial, or commercial purposes; or the proceeds of which have been used, or are to be used, for such purposes. . . ." It also gives the Federal Reserve Board the power "to determine or define the character of the paper eligible for discount, within the meaning of the Act." Certain specific kinds of loans are excluded, namely purely speculative and long-term loans.

The term "self-liquidating" is not part of the explicit language of the act. Nor is there any statement to the effect that if attention is paid to asset quality—that is, self-liquidating loans—bank liquidity will be guaranteed. The language of the act is neutral with respect to a strong real bills interpretation. Stripped of its strong real bills interpretation, the doctrine is innocuous. Its deliberate vagueness turned out to be its strength, for rival interpretations could more easily be accommodated.

The evidence for the influence of the real bills doctrine can also be found in the views of the framers of the act. Parker Willis, who drafted the Glass bill, was an ardent supporter of the real bills theory, as was his mentor J. Lawrence Laughlin of the University of Chicago. According to West (1977, pp. 64–67): "Willis and others viewed the Federal Reserve Act as legislating the real bills doctrine as a policy guide," and he maintained that the "law accepts the banking theory of the note issue rather than the so-called currency theory." Friedman and Schwartz (1963, p. 193) also stated that the real bills doctrine was incorporated in the Federal Reserve Act *albeit in limited form*. However, there were others who played minor roles and who were active in the banking reform movement and were followers of the real bills doctrine including Horace White (1911), Charles A. Conant (1905), J. Lawrence Laughlin (1903), and William A. Scott (1903).

The evidence of the influence of the real bills doctrine derives less from an interpretation of the provisions of the Federal Reserve Act and more from the behavior of Fed policymakers in the system's formative years. Policymakers in the early years may have been strongly influenced by real bills in at least two important episodes: the reluctance to raise discount rates in 1919 to curb inflation and a similar reluctance to raise rates to forestall stock market speculation in 1928 and 1929. Emphasis was directed at the quality of credit and not the quantity. The famous *Tenth Annual Report* of the Federal Reserve Board has also been interpreted as a real bills manifesto. It was probably drafted by Board member Adolph Miller, who had been a colleague of Laughlin's at the University of Chicago.

The report proposed both a qualitative and a quantitative test for an excess supply of credit. The real bills influence is apparent in the exposition of the qualitative test (Tenth Annual Report, p. 145):

> The Federal Reserve System is a system of productive credit. It is not a system of credit for either investment or speculative purposes. Credit in the service of agriculture, industry, and trade may be described comprehensively as credit for productive use. The exclusion of the use of Federal Reserve credit for speculative and industrial purposes and its limitation to agricultural, industrial, or commercial purposes thus clearly indicates the nature of the tests which are appropriate as guides in the extension of Federal reserve credit.

The report also proposed an alternative test—a quantitative test—that justified an increase in the amount of credit if it was accompanied by a commensurate increase in the nation's aggregate productivity (output). Given the availability of production indices, it was fairly simple to administer.

Mints (1945, pp. 266–67) described the two tests but dismissed the second on the mistaken grounds that the Board thought the first would be sufficient. The significance of both tests is emphasized in its Annual Report (1924, pp. 33–34).

> The Board is fully aware of the fact that the problem of credit exten-
> sion involves the question of amount or volume as well as the ques-
> tion of kind or character; otherwise stated involves a *quantitative* as
> well as a *qualitative* determination. But it is the view of the Board
> that it is not necessary to go outside the Federal reserve act to find
> suitable methods of estimating the adjustment of the volume of cred-
> it provided by the Federal Reserve banks to the volume of credit
> needs. The Federal Reserve Act itself suggests the nature of the tests,
> guides, or indicators, whatever they may be called to be used in gaug-
> ing the need for and the adequacy of Federal Reserve credit.

The quantitative test revealed that the Board was aware that price inflation might ensue if credit expansion continued that was not accompanied
by a commensurate increase in output. Effective applications of the quantitative test were made in 1922–23 (Wicker, 1966, chapter 5). The behavior of Fed policymakers in the formative years is not consistent with the
claim that they were committed to the strong form of the real bills
doctrine.

Our sole concern in this chapter is the language of the Glass-Owen and
Aldrich bills and what can be inferred about real bills influence. Briefly,
our conclusion is that the language of the Federal Reserve Act is neutral,
that is, consistent with either the acceptance or repudiation of the real bills
doctrine. A comparison of the Aldrich and Glass-Owen bills has revealed
a similarity of wording in the discount provision that was not accidental.
However, the implications of this striking parallelism have been overlooked. According to West (1977, p. 155) the real bills doctrine was the
cornerstone of the Federal Reserve Act. But the Aldrich bill was free from
such an association and did not evoke the same criterion. Carter Glass and
Parker Willis were proponents of real bills, but at least two, if not three, of
the five Jekyll Island participants specifically repudiated it. Neither bill
contained language explicitly related to the strongest form of that doctrine. Banking theory considerations may have influenced Willis, but the
discount provisions of the Aldrich bill were drawn from the practice of the
Reichsbank. Therefore, the language of the two bills was real bills neutral,
though their underpinning may have differed substantially.

We know what it means to claim that those who drafted the Federal
Reserve Act accepted the theories of the banking school, but what did

Willis mean when he said the law accepts the banking school theory of the note issue? How can the law accept a particular banking theory? Suppose that all of our sources concerning the origins of the Federal Reserve Act were suddenly destroyed and the only thing that remained was the test of the act itself. What can we infer from reading and interpreting the act about how the real bills doctrine influenced specific provisions of the act, namely those dealing with discounting and the issue of notes?

We reproduced in part Section 13 of the Federal Reserve Act a few pages earlier. To reveal evidences of real bills in Section 13 we need to review the characteristic features of that doctrine:

1. Short-term commercial paper is the desired asset in the port-folios of both the commercial banks and the central bank.
2. The property that makes it desirable is its alleged self-liquidating feature.
3. Purely speculative loans and long-term loans for investment purposes are excluded.
4. The note issue is self-regulating.

Points one and three are included in Section 13. The emphasis accorded short-term commercial paper is a necessary but not sufficient condition for the validity of the strong form of the real bills doctrine. The self-liquidating feature does not appear in the language of the act, nor is there any statement to the effect that the note issue is self-regulating. There is no internal evidence that the real bills doctrine in its fallacious form appears in the original act.

In a purely hypothetical real bills model where individual banks issued paper currency, there is no role for a central bank. The problem of bank liquidity does not arise since liquidity allegedly is guaranteed, if, that is, bank lending is confined to self-liquidating commercial paper. Moreover, currency notes issued by the banks are self-regulating. Ergo, in such a strict real bills model there would be no banking panics. The solution to the bank instability problem therefore was to constrain asset quality of the commercial banks. Nevertheless, advocates of real bills were not deterred from advocating a central bank. They simply were not prepared to push the purely hypothetical real bills model to its limits. The proposal to allow banks to create an asset-based currency had been rejected, as well as a bond-secured currency established by the National Banking Act. In its place the banking reformers substituted an asset-based paper currency issued by a central bank backed 100 percent by commercial paper. The central bank did not intend to control the amount of currency supplied. Presumably it would be demand determined.

The absence of specific policy guides like the money stock and prices in the Federal Reserve Act has puzzled historians of the Fed. A purely passive stance with respect to these variables is at least consistent with such an omission. The framers of the act took it for granted that the gold standard was the long-run determinant of the money stock.

Nor does the Federal Reserve Act spell out the circumstances when the discount rate should be changed. Real bills had nothing to say about discount rate behavior. Both the congressional hearings and the debates show an awareness that discount rate changes should influence gold flows and the level of economic activity.

The criterion to access the discount window was the availability of eligible paper. According to Harris (1933, p. 297) eligibility criteria were framed with a view to stimulating the use of self-liquidating paper of a commercial type. However, by 1925 no clearly defined criteria of eligibility had emerged, which led Willis (1923, p. 905) to conclude that it was "almost impossible to lay down any definite standard of 'eligibility' which should be universally applied in all districts." Reliance on the discretion of Reserve Bank officials in the absence of any instrument necessarily introduced a note of uncertainty with respect to the availability of reserves and never provided the sense of absolute security characteristic of the German discount market with its standardized financial instrument. The sense of insecurity was greatest during the period of direct pressure during 1928–29 when officials attempted to control the flow of credit to the stock market. By 1933, Harris (1933, Vol. 1, p. 286) noted that member banks in financial centers obtained most of their advances by borrowing on their own notes instead of commercial paper.

REAL BILLS AND THE ALDRICH PLAN

Section 26 of the Aldrich bill reads as follows: "The National Reserve Association may through a branch rediscount for and with the endorsement of any bank having a deposit with it, notes and bills of exchange arising out of commercial transaction, that is, notes and bills of exchange issued or drawn for agricultural, industrial, or commercial purposes, and not including notes of bills issued or drawn for the purpose of carrying stocks, bonds, or other investment securities." This section of the Aldrich bills is almost identical in wording to Section 13 of the Federal Reserve Act.

The discount provision of the Aldrich bill was identical to Glass-Owen, but the underpinnings were radically different. The Aldrich bill's discount provision was modeled after the German prototype as understood by Paul

Warburg and grounded in his banking experience in Germany before his move to the United States in 1902. At the center of the German system was a highly organized discount market almost totally absent in this country, where bills of exchange were freely traded in an open market among the different issuers, the Credit Banks and the Reichsbank. The bill of exchange was a standardized financial instrument whose main characteristics were: (1) it bore the endorsement or acceptance by a well-established bank; (2) it was highly liquid and of short maturity, saleable at any time in an organized market; and (3) it was subject to uniform laws governing such paper. The bill of exchange was self-liquidating, though not automatically in the classical real bills sense. Emphasis was placed upon bills of short maturity where the expected proceeds of the sale of the goods would be used to repay the loan. Quality alone was never the sole criterion for judging safety. Of equal importance was the reputation of the endorsers and acceptors, and the existence of a robust market for commercial paper. According to Warburg (1930, Vol. 2, p. 223) it was Germany's highly developed discount system that averted banking panics "with as much certainty as we may expect their occurrence with us."

The alleged success of the German discount system can be attributed to a combination of circumstances: (1) the existence of a uniform and standardized financial instrument; (2) an efficient discount market; (3) a central bank; (4) a highly concentrated banking structure with numerous decentralized branches; and (5) the proportion of cash-using to deposit-using transactions was still relatively large compared with the United States and Britain. Warburg tended to stress points 1–3 to account for the absence of banking panics in Germany, but he ignored 4 and 5. He was well aware of the importance of the highly concentrated branch banking system in Germany. Item five, particularly, has not been sufficiently emphasized. The proportion of cash- to deposit-using transactions was still very large in Germany, certainly much larger, for example, than in the United States and Great Britain. Savings deposits were concentrated in specialized banks known as *Sparkassen* where deposits were guaranteed and notice of withdrawal could be requested. Cash-using transactions were concentrated among the holders of savings deposits. The conclusion we might draw is deposits in the Sparkassen were not a likely source of unexpected deposit withdrawals in time of uncertainty.

Deposits of Berlin Credit Banks were estimated in 1908 to be between 3 and 3.5 billion marks ($8.8 million). There were also Cooperative Banks with more than 2.3 billion marks. In all of Germany deposits may have totaled more than 8 billion marks, or $2 billion. By way of comparison deposits in New York banks amounted to $10 billion. Deposits of the large Credit Banks were mainly deposits of large industrial establishments, and the Reichsbank transferred claims among the Credit Banks by means of book credits, thereby reducing the business demand for check-using transactions.

Unanticipated deposit withdrawals of excited small depositors of the Sparkassen were less likely than in the United States to ignite bank contagion. Moreover, the size, composition, and distribution of deposits payable on demand made German banks less prone to unexpected deposit withdrawals. German banks were not as vulnerable to deposit shocks as U.S. banks. And deposit guarantees at the Sparkassen may have contributed to relative deposit stability in periods of nascent banking unrest.

The real bills doctrine was not the source for the role accorded commercial paper in the Aldrich bill. Warburg was a practical banker with only a peripheral interest in banking theory. Although he never referred directly to the real bills doctrine, he disparaged those who treated bank credit or the note issue as self-regulating or automatic in its ebb and flow. Employing the metaphor of water flows, Warburg (1930, Vol. 2, p. 128) regarded as the duty of the central bank to supply legitimate credit demands. He added: "No automation—no tax or fixed regulator—can perform it, but the best judgment of the best experts must indicate the policy to be pursued from time to time." Similarly he argued that currency notes should expand and contract in accord with the requirements of trade: "However, this is not a merely automatic process when those entrusted with the management of the central bank see the necessity of exercising a restraining influence on the business community, they raise the rate at which the bank will discount . . ."

A. Piatt Andrew, who also attended the Jekyll Island meeting, regarded the real bills doctrine in its strictest form as fallacious. He (1904, p. 16) maintained that it was "preposterous then to assume that credit can be issued indefinitely upon the basis of goods without any regard whatever to the quantity of available money in which it is likely from time to time to be expected for redemption." He also recognized that as prices rose, the demand for credit would lead to a race between credit expansion and prices.

The discount provisions of the Aldrich and Glass-Owen bills were identical. Yet at least two if not three of the framers of the Aldrich bill had rejected the real bills doctrine as fallacious.

West (1977, p. 150) concluded that it was remarkable that the two sides could agree on the same discount provisions with such strong contrasting views on the validity of the real bills doctrine. A comparison of the discount provisions of the two bills reveals that the Federal Reserve Act was neutral with respect to the strong form of real bills. There was nothing within the act itself to discriminate between a Warburg-Andrew and a Glass-Willis interpretation of that same provision.

We are perhaps in a better position to answer our initial question: What did Willis mean when he said the law accepts the banking school theory of the note issue? The law neither accepted nor rejected the banking school theory; it was consistent with both its acceptance and its rejection, that is, it was neutral!

CHAPTER NINE

EPILOGUE

During the past fifteen years there has been a reawakening of interest in what can be called the origins of the Fed question. I include in that phrase not only the reasons for the establishment of a U.S. style central bank but also remedies, politically feasible and infeasible, that were rejected. There were many banking reform proposals considered, including branch banking, deposit insurance, an asset-based currency, reserve pooling by the NYCH banks, and a central bank. Asset-based currency proposals were sometimes coupled with branch banking and deposit insurance provisions. One version of the Glass-Owen bill creating the Fed contained a provision for deposit insurance. Two of these schemes received far more attention than the others. The asset-based currency proposals dominated the first stage of the movement for banking reform from 1894 to 1908. And a central bank monopolized the second and third stages from 1908 until the passage of the Federal Reserve Act in 1913.

Historians generally have been slow to show an interest in the origins of the Fed question. McCulley and Livingston were exceptions. Using the archival records including the papers of the leading participants, they reexamined the first stage of the debate on banking reform. We gave a brief description and evaluation of their contributions in chapter 2. Political scientists have also only recently discovered the Fed. The politics of the Fed was, they thought, too important to be left to economists. Broz attributed the origins of the Fed to international considerations, playing down the controversial role assigned to domestic factors. New York bankers, in his analysis, overcame their reluctance for collective action by weighing the anticipated benefits and losses that would accrue from the new role of the United States as international bankers with the creation of a central bank.

Admirable as the McCulley and Livingston studies are, they both fall short of drawing any inferences about the contribution of Senator Nelson Aldrich to the establishment of the Federal Reserve System. They give adequate treatment to the Aldrich-Vreeland and the Aldrich bills but failed to acknowledge the Aldrich legacy of providing the underpinnings for the creation of the Fed. It was Aldrich and Carter Glass who made the case successfully for a U.S. style central bank and who drafted bills, most if not all the provisions of which were reproduced both in substance and wording in the Glass-Owen bill. Aldrich won the battle for a central bank, while Glass succeeded in steering the legislation for a central bank through Congress—from which I infer that Aldrich is deserving of the accolade, co-founder of the Fed.

The Federal Reserve Act had its origin in the growing dissatisfaction generated by the performance of the banking and monetary system under the National Banking Act, the sources of which were readily acknowledged—an inelastic currency, lack of emergency reserves, and no effective mechanism for promoting cooperation among the banks. Agitation for banking reform accelerated after the banking panic of 1893, slowly at first by spreading to concerned interest groups, especially bankers and businessmen acting through national associations that served both as a platform for reform proposals and a pulpit for their dissemination.

The movement for banking reform in the first two stages I have referred to as the Great Debate. Its precise dating was entirely arbitrary; it seemed a convenient point to begin the narrative when the debate became national in scope. That is not meant, however, to denigrate the significance of the contributions of numerous individual critics in the years prior to 1893. For the purpose of organizing the narrative and imparting a sense of unity and coherence to the numerous banking reform proposals, I divided the period into three separate but overlapping stages. The first stage from 1894 to 1908 culminated in the Aldrich-Vreeland Act (1908) and was dominated by asset-based currency proposals. A U.S. style central bank monopolized the second and third stages and ended with the passage of the Federal Reserve Act in 1913.

To establish a central bank in the U.S. we explained how at least three formidable obstacles had to be removed. The first was the shibboleth against a central bank, the legacy of Andrew Jackson's feud with Nicholas Biddle over the renewal of the charter of the Second Bank of the United States. The First and Second Banks of the United States performed some central banking functions, and their demise left a traumatic residue that was one of the chief obstacles to the creation of the Fed. Timberlake (1978) attempted to answer the question: What were the origins of central banking in the United States? This is not to be confused with the narrower question: What were the origins of the Federal Reserve System? At the time of the Great Debate opposition to a central bank was a political fact of life. To remove this obstacle was a precondition for the creation of a U.S. style central bank.

There were two other obstacles. Asset-based currency proposals had gained a wide acceptability among bankers and businessmen during the first stage of the Great Debate. Their appeal resided in the fact that there was no need for a fundamental reconstruction of the banking system. The third obstacle was the absence of either presidential or congressional leadership on this issue at least before 1908. We attributed the removal of this stumbling block to Senator Nelson Aldrich when he became chairman of the National Monetary Commission. The transition from an asset-based currency as embodied in the Aldrich-Vreeland Act to a central bank as proposed in the Aldrich bill occurred within the short space of three years. It was during this stage that a handful of distinguished and articulate Wall Street bankers seized the initiative from Chicago and Midwestern bankers and shifted the debate on banking reform from an asset-based currency to a European style central bank adapted to U.S. banking experience. And it was Senator Aldrich whose leadership was responsible for this sweeping change in the course of banking reform. The abruptness of the shift in the debate to a central bank requires an explanation. To attribute the change to the deliberations of the National Monetary Commission would be to conceal more than it reveals. Senator Aldrich was the Monetary Commission. What was done was done at his initiative with consultation with commission members only after the fact. Moreover, there is no surviving evidence that the commission ever considered seriously any alternative to a central bank. Aldrich became a convert to a central bank during his visit to Europe in the summer of 1908. As far as he was concerned, the issue of a central bank was settled. The only task that remained was to formulate a concrete plan of a U.S. style central bank. Without the knowledge of commission members, Aldrich proceeded to assemble a select group of Wall Street bankers who were sympathetic to the idea of a central bank for the purpose of preparing a rough draft of a bill. The only economist who was a participant was A. Piatt Andrew.

We did not learn who these Wall Street bankers were until 1930 when Aldrich's biographer revealed their names. Though well known in Wall Street, they were less well known to the general public. Only one of the three banker participants at Jekyll Island had any direct knowledge or experience of central banking in Europe, and that was Paul Warburg. Why, we may ask, did Aldrich bypass the commission when drafting a bill? And why was it done in a clandestine manner? Here we can only conjecture. He may have thought the eighteen-member commission too cumbersome a body for the delicate task of framing a bill. His experience in the Senate may have taught him that too many cooks spoil the pudding! Or he may simply have had no confidence that commission members could perform the task. Once Aldrich had decided that this was a task for

Wall Street bankers, he knew that they would have no credibility in the country as a whole if their names were revealed. He was prepared to accept the risk that if the public learned of their existence, his credibility would be lost.

The clandestine meeting at Jekyll Island in November 1910 establishes the fact that a cabal of Wall Street bankers formulated and drafted the earliest version of the Aldrich bill. Can their influence have extended to the Glass-Owen bill as well? If it did, the channel of influence would be through the Aldrich bill. Glass and Willis, as we have stated many times, never tired of claiming that the two bills were separate and distinct with little or no connection between them. Warburg (1930) attempted to refute their claim more than seventy-five years ago, apparently with little success judging by the eclipse of Aldrich and the role he played in the establishment of a U.S. central bank. A line-by-line comparison of the provisions of both bills reveals a striking similarity in both substance and wording, though not in all provisions. Warburg took the comparison as convincing evidence of how heavily Glass-Owen leaned directly on the Aldrich bill in its formulation and indirectly on the Wall Street bankers who drafted the Aldrich bill. It is indeed anomalous that in a country with a well-documented antipathy to Wall Street control, Wall Street bankers at Jekyll Island were responsible for designing a U.S. style central bank. Aldrich himself thought he had dispelled the specter of Wall Street control through instilling into the organization of the National Reserve Association the two principles of federalism and democratic control.

Broz also assigned a key role to the New York bankers, more inclusive than the Jekyll Island cabal. They were motivated, in his opinion, purely by international considerations, mainly to support the internationalization of the dollar. According to Broz, a handful of New York bankers who could take advantage of internationalizing the dollar had a strong economic incentive to initiate a plan for banking reform that would enable the dollar to acquire the status of an international currency. These New York bankers successfully achieved their objective, but despite themselves they vigorously objected to the Glass-Owen bill.

At the very outset we identified three propositions about the origins of the Fed that deserved reconsideration:

1. Carter Glass and his associate Parker Willis were solely responsible for drafting and steering the Federal Reserve Act through Congress.
2. Panic prevention was its main objective.
3. The real bills doctrine was the theoretical underpinning for the Federal Reserve Act.

We have attempted to show that Senator Nelson Aldrich and Glass deserve equal billing as founders of the Fed. To support that claim we made a detailed comparison of the provisions of both the Aldrich and Glass-Owen bills and also cited as additional evidence Warburg's line-by-line comparison of their substance and wording. Moreover, it was Aldrich, not Glass, who turned the movement for banking reform away from asset-based currency proposals to a central bank. It was Aldrich and not Glass who successfully confronted the national prejudice against a central bank inherited from the Jackson-Biddle debate earlier in the eighteenth century. Aldrich's legacy enabled Glass to concentrate solely on the purely technical questions in drafting an alternative to the rejected Aldrich bill.

Panic prevention did not require the creation of a central bank. The emergency asset-based currency proposal provided for in the Aldrich-Vreeland Act successfully aborted the incipient banking panic in 1914. The evidence to support this hypothesis was contained in our detailed analysis of that banking crisis.

The Federal Reserve Act itself cannot sustain a strong real bills interpretation. The substance and wording of the discount provisions of both the Aldrich and Glass bills are almost identical. At least three of the Jekyll Island cabal that drafted an outline of the Aldrich bill regarded the real bills doctrine as fallacious, whereas Glass and Willis were committed to the real bills view. The substance and wording of the discount provision is therefore consistent with its acceptance and rejection! From which I concluded the Federal Reserve Act was real bills neutral.

This concludes our story of the origins of the Fed. The Great Debate on banking reform has all but been forgotten. We know that the debate was about a central bank, but we no longer remember who the adversaries were. There was not simply opposition to a central bank but a set of specific asset-based currency proposals that had been debated beginning with the Baltimore Plan in 1894 and ending with the Aldrich-Vreeland bill in 1908. The Aldrich-Vreeland Act had resolved at least two of the main problems of the national banking system: an emergency currency and prevention of banking panics. But the act was not meant to be permanent; it was due to expire in 1914, to be replaced by the recommendations of the National Monetary Commission. Why then was it necessary to create a central bank? The answer resides in the leadership of Senator Nelson Aldrich when he assumed chairmanship of the commission. He was chiefly responsible for shifting attention away from an asset-based currency to the idea of a central bank. Aldrich became a convert to a central bank in the summer of 1908 when the commission visited European central banks. Thereafter the only issue on the table was: What kind of central bank? Even after the Aldrich plan for a central bank had been rejected,

Glass accepted the necessity of a central bank and proceeded to build on the foundations laid by Aldrich and his associates, even if he never tired of denying the connection. We have attempted to explain why the Federal Reserve Act owes as much, if not more, to Senator Nelson Aldrich as it does to Representative Carter Glass. And the acknowledgment of that debt has been long overdue. Moreover, absent Aldrich, we do not know how close we came to adopting an asset-based currency. The creation of a U.S. style central bank was in a very real sense almost an accident!

REFERENCES

PRIMARY

Aldrich Bill (Aldrich-Vreeland), 1908. Sen. 3023 Banking and Currency Committee, 60th Congress, 1st Session.

American Bankers Association, 1907. ABA Currency Proposal. Proceedings of the 33rd Annual Convention of ABA, New York.

Baltimore Plan, American Banking Association *Proceedings,* October 1894.

Chamber of Commerce of State of New York, 1906. Currency Report, New York.

Indianapolis Monetary Commission, 1898. Report of Monetary Commission to Executive Committee.

Indianapolis Monetary Commission, 1898. A History of the Movement for the Monetary Commission. Indianapolis January 12 and 13 and Report of Its Proceedings.

Indianapolis Monetary Convention, 1900. Report of the Monetary Commission of the Indianapolis Convention. Hollenbeck Press, Indianapolis.

"Suggested Plan for Monetary Legislation Submitted to the National Monetary Commission," rev. ed., 1911. S. Doc 784, Part 2. 61st Congress, 3rd sess. 1911. Washington, DC: U.S. Government Printing Office.

U.S. Congress, House of Representatives, 1894. Hearings on HR 8149, 53rd Congress, 3rd Session.

Tenth Annual Report of the Board of Governors of the Federal Reserve System, 1924. Washington, D.C.

U.S. Congress, House of Representatives, 1908. Hearings and Arguments on Proposed Currency Legislation, Aldrich Bill, 60th Congress, 1st Session.

SECONDARY

Aldrich, Nelson W., 1911. *Suggested Plan for Monetary Legislation,* submitted to the National Monetary Commission, S. Doc. 784, 61st Congress, 3rd Session, Government Printing Office, Washington.

————, *Suggested Plan for Monetary Legislation,* submitted to National Monetary Commission, revised edition, S. Doc. 784, Part 2, 61st Congress, 3rd Session, 1911.

Andrew, A. Piatt, 1904, *Credit and the Value of Money.* Also publication: Paper and Proceedings, American Economic Association, 6 (February 1905).

Broz, J. Lawrence, 1997. *The International Origins of the Federal Reserve System,* Cornell University Press, Ithaca and London.

Byrnes, James F., 1912. *Congressional Record,* Vol. 48, Pt. 6, 62nd Congress, 2nd Session, Washington.

Carlisle, John G., 1894. Report of the Committee on Banking and Currency Together with Hearings. House of Representatives, 8149, 53rd Congress, 3rd Session.

Case, Everett, 1934. Notes on Interview with A. Piatt Andrew, Thursday, February 1. Made available by Andrew Gray to author.

Chandler, Lester, 1958. *Benjamin Strong.* Brookings Institution, Washington.

Conant, Charles, 1905. *The Principles of Money and Banking.* Harper & Brothers, New York.

Dunbar, Charles F., 1907. *Chapters on the Theory and History of Banking.* G.P. Putnam and Sons, New York.

Eckels, James H., 1894. Report of the Committee on Banking and Currency Together with Hearings. House of Representatives 8149, 53rd Congress, 3rd Session.

————, 1894. Annual Report of the Comptroller of the Currency, 3rd Session, 53rd Congress, Dec. 3. Government Printing Office, Washington.

Forgan, James, 1908. House Hearings on Senate bill 3023, Banking and Currency Committee. 60th Congress, 1st Session, House of Representatives, Washington.

Fowler, Charles H., 1906. HR 23017, 59th Congress, 2nd Session.

Friedman, Milton, and Anna Schwartz, 1963. *A Monetary History of the United States,* Princeton University Press, Princeton, NJ.

Glass, Carter, 1927. *An Adventure in Constructive Finance,* Doubleday, Garden City, NJ.

Gorton, Gary, 1985. "Clearing Houses and the Origin of Central Banking in the United States," *The Journal of Economic History* 45 (June): 277–83.

Gorton, Gary, and D. Mulleneaux, 1987. "The Joint Production of Confidence, Endogenous Regulation and Nineteenth Century Commercial Bank Clearinghouses," *Journal of Money, Credit and Banking,* Vol. 19, No. 5 (November): 457–68.

Gray, Andrew, 1971. "Who Killed the Aldrich Plan?" *The Bankers Magazine* 54 (Summer): 62–74.

Harris, Seymore, 1933. *Twenty Years of Federal Reserve Policy,* 2 Vols., Harvard University Press, Cambridge.

Lamont, Thomas W., 1933. *Henry P. Davison,* Harper and Brothers, London.

Laughlin, J. Lawrence, 1903. *The Principles of Money.* New York.

———, 1908, The Currency Problem and the Present Financial Situation, Columbia University Press, New York.

———, 1920. *Banking Progress,* Charles Scribners, New York.

Livingston, James, 1986. *Origins of the Federal Reserve System,* Cornell University Press, Ithaca and London.

McCulley, Richard T., 1992. *Banks and Politics During the Progressive Era. The Origins of the Federal Reserve System, 1897–1913.* Garland Publishing, New York.

Mints, Lloyd W., 1945. *A History of Banking Theory,* University of Chicago Press, Chicago.

Morawetz, Victor, 1909. *The Banking and Currency Problem in the United States,* North American Review Publishing Co., New York.

———, 1908, House Hearings on Senate 3023 Banking and Currency Committee, 60th Congress, 1st Session, House of Representatives, Washington.

———, 1911. "The Banking and Currency Problem in the United States." Proceedings of the Academy of Political Science, *The Reform of the Currency.* Ed. Henry David Mussey. The Academy of Political Science. New York: Columbia University Press, pp. 343–57.

Muhleman, Maurice, 1909, 1910. "A Plan For a Central Bank," *Banking Law Journal* (Nov. and Dec. 1909 and January-February 1910).

Pratt, Orville, 1903. Senate bill S2716.

Scott, William A., 1903. *Money and Banking,* 2nd ed. New York.

———, 1913. *Money.* A.C. McClurg, Chicago.

Smith, Rixey, and Norman Beasley, 1939. *Carter Glass.* Longman, Green, New York.

Seligman, E.R.A. 1908. *The Currency Problem and the Present Financial Situation.* Columbia University Press, New York.

Sprague, Oliver M.W., 1910. *History of Crises under the National Banking System.* Washington, DC: U.S. Government Printing Office.

———, 1911. *Banking Reform in the United States.* Cambridge: Harvard University Press.

———, 1914. "The War and the Financial Situation in the United States," *Quarterly Journal of Economics* 29 (November): 181–86.

———, 1915. "The Crisis of 1914 in the United States," *American Economic Review* 5 (September): 499–533.

Stephenson, Nathaniel Wright, 1930. *Nelson Aldrich,* Charles Scribners, New York.

Tallman, Ellis, and Jon R. Moen, 1990. "Lessons from the Panic of 1907." Federal Reserve Bank of St. Louis. *Economic Review* (May/June): 2–13

————, 2001. "An Alternative Explanation for the Establishment of a Central Bank." Unpublished manuscript.

Timberlake, Richard H., Jr., 1978. *The Origins of Central Banking in the United States,* Harvard University Press, Cambridge.

————, 1984. "The Central Banking Role of Clearinghouse Associations." *Journal of Money, Credit, and Banking* 16, no. 1 (February 1984): 1–15.

————, 1993. *Monetary Policy in the United States.* Chicago: University of Chicago Press.

Toma, Mark, 1997. *Competition and Monopoly in the Federal Reserve System 1914–1951.* Cambridge University Press, Cambridge.

Vanderlip, Frank A., and Boyden Sparks, 1935. *From Farm Boy to Financier,* Appleton-Century, New York.

Warburg, Paul M., 1914. *Essays on Banking Reform in the United States.* Proceedings of the Academy of Political Science, 4, no. 4 (July).

————. 1930. *The Federal Reserve System,* 2 volumes, Macmillan, New York.

West, Robert Craig, 1977. *Banking Reform and the Federal Reserve, 1863–1927,* Cornell University Press, Ithaca and London.

White, Horace, 1911. *Money and Banking,* 4th edition, Ginn & Co., Boston.

Wicker, Elmus, 1966. *Federal Reserve Monetary Policy, 1917–1933,* Random House, New York.

————, 1996. "Were Banking Panics of the National Banking Era Preventable?" Unpublished manuscript.

————, 2000. *Banking Panics of the Gilded Age,* Cambridge University Press, Cambridge.

Willis, H. Parker, 1923. *The Federal Reserve System,* Ronald Press, New York.

INDEX